THE COMMON SENSE APPROACH TO
A HEALTHY RELATIONSHIP

LOVE, SEX AND SPIRITUALITY

Written by
Albert John Murphy

THE COMMON SENSE APPROACH TO
A HEALTHY RELATIONSHIP

LOVE, SEX AND SPIRITUALITY

Written by
Albert John Murphy

Self-Published with help from
Midnight Express Books

The Common Sense Approach to A Healthy Relationship
LOVE, SEX AND SPIRITUALITY

Copyright©2015 Albert John Murphy
ISBN-13: 978-0692420027 (Midnight Express Books)
ISBN-10: 0692420029

Cover idea by The Purple Monkey

Cover design & layout by Midnight Express Books

Self-Published with help from
Midnight Express Books
POBox 69
Berryville AR 72616
(870) 210-3772
MEBooks1@yahoo.com

THE COMMON SENSE APPROACH TO
A HEALTHY RELATIONSHIP

LOVE, SEX AND SPIRITUALITY

Written by
Albert John Murphy

ACKNOWLEDGMENTS

First and foremost, I want to thank yah – the Creator and the Crown Brothers and Sisters in Israel, and to the saints.

My daughter, Rokyah, has been my inspiration; I love you baby.

My mother, Paula; bless your name. You are my backbone.

My nephew, Boom Boom. I love you; I'm doing this for us!

My brother, Bobby, and my sister, Sharlane, thank you. I know that y'all watching over me from heaven. Y'all my angels.

And to my brother John, I love you man.

My Grandmother, Earnestine, thank you for giving me wisdom, love, and support through the years.

And to my cuz, sister Victoria, thank you. You believed in my dreams when no one else did. I love you.

Marshelia, thank you for encouraging me when I was feeling sorry for myself.

I want to thank my good friend John Ebert for putting up with my craziness.

I want to thank "Purple Monky" for drawing me a cool cover.

Thank you Linda and Victor Huddleston at Midnight Express Books for being patient with me and for creating one of the coolest publishing companies in the world!

Those that I didn't mention, you know who you are. Thank you for your love and support.

R.I.P. Ben Ammi my spiritual leader; I love you.

Albert Murphy

INTRODUCTION

The common sense approach is a healthy and effective way to handle relationship, family, friends and business affairs. "The Common Sense Philosophy" provides the reader with an arsenal of information. It provides a high moral, high value plan to achieve a healthy relationship. It has information to help improve your sex life and much more. I pray and hope that you enjoy the book.

Yours Truly,

Albert Murphy

PREFACE

How well matched are you and your partner? Here's a guide to hotter sex.

This is an article taken from the September 2008 Men's Health magazine. Mismatched socks are tolerable. Mismatched sex is not. Avoid these five common sexual disconnects—and find the right fit with any woman.

1. HER AROUSAL is at a slow burn, but you're raring to go. Sure, women are typically slower than men at becoming sexually amped. "But it actually takes much less time than even woman realize," says Scott Haltzman, M.D., author of *The Secrets of Happily Married Men.* Rig the system: If you reinforce the idea that she's aroused it may happen more quickly. Tell her you see that her nipples are hard and you feel she's wet. Her brain will signal her body to feel that desire, Haltzman says.

2. You like dirty talk, but she's timid. Just because she's keeping quiet, don't assume she's opposed to sex talk. "A woman may not like to talk dirty because it takes her away from her body and sensations," says Joy Davidson, Ph.D., a New York based

sex therapist and the author of *Fearless Sex*. But she might really like it if you talk dirty to her. Feed her lines while you're teasing her. Ask her what she wants you to do next. During sex, ask her what she likes best about how it feels. "In the future, she'll have those phrases on hand," Davidson says.

3. You always make the first move. "Women may subconsciously feel they need permission to take the lead," says Patti Britton, Ph.D. author of *The Art of Sex Coaching*. Casually say I wonder what it'd be like if you took the lead tonight. That would really turn me on. "Also, realize that any of her casual comments about sex or anything about either your body or hers, are often subtle requests," Haltzman says.

4. Your number is higher than hers. "A big gap in backroom know how can make her worry about her performance or about being just another brick in the well," says Haltzman. In that case. "Don't rush in with your whole utility belt of sexual experience and toys," he says. Face-to-face positions, cowboy (a.k.a. cowgirl), missionary sitting together on a chair, are best, because they offer her a sense of intimacy and connection. And forget about the Big O at first. Focusing on orgasm only stresses her.

5. The two of you don't measure up. If there's a significant height difference between the two of you, furniture can be your best

friend. If she's taller, try lying on an ottoman or a small bench and have her straddle you. "That way she can still have her feet on the ground," Haltzman says, "giving her leverage and flexibility."

"Or, if you're taller, try holding her up and pinning her against the wall," says Brian Zamboni, Ph.D., a sex therapist and clinical psychologist at the University of Minnesota.

Contents

CHAPTER 1 What to Look For in a Mate

Women, in general are a few steps ahead of most men. If you are confused, and don't know what to look for in a spouse, I will discuss a few things to look for in a spouse. A woman has five (5) basic needs.

1. *Provider*—A man who can provide for his family and his women represent strength, and stability. We now live in the days of the independent woman. And most women are the providers. There is not too many women who delight in a guy who is broke. I personally think it's very important for a man to be financially stable. Seventy percent of relationships and marriages end—or are badly damaged from money problems. Money is not everything, and if two human beings love one another, it's important to have a dream, and support each other's dreams, and encourage and help achieve one another's goals.

2. *Communication*—Men communicate different from women. For instance, a man comes home from work. He goes to the refrigerator. He grabs a nice cool beer and takes a seat. He has had a long hard day. He had an altercation with his boss, and he does not know if he lost his job. He goes in a "shell" or a

cave. Meaning, he is not talking much. He keeps quiet and stays to himself. His wife asked him, "Honey, what's wrong? How was your day at work?" And he says, "It was cool."

Women communicate differently. If a woman has a bad day at work, or at school, she will come home and tell her spouse everything that happened. When a woman purges her conscious of her troubles, her body releases hormones to relieve the stress. We must be honest, open and clear in our communication. Our families and spouses are not mind readers.

3. *Listen*—It's very important to listen. I have learned from past relationships that women just want her man to listen to her. Many people confuse listening from hearing. I can hear what a person is saying to me, but my mind is somewhere else. Listening is defined by Webster's dictionary as: Pay attention in order to hear.

    In past relationships my girlfriend criticized me for not listening. So guys if you want the ladies, you don't have to run game on them. Just be quiet and listen. Encourage your lady to talk and you listen. I will talk more about this subject in a later chapter.

4. *Physical Strength*—I believe every human being desires a healthy spouse. It's important to maintain a healthy lifestyle.

Maintain a balanced diet. Become active and exercise. Exercise releases hormones that tame stress in the body. A poor diet and stress is the number one cause of high blood pressure and stroke and diabetes. Diet and exercise has also been known to improve sex and stamina, which is very important in relationship and marriage. Studies have shown that people who are physically fit, have higher self-esteem. And women feel more secure around strong, healthy men.

5. *Education*—This is a tool that allows an individual to be free. I can tell a person to fly an airplane, but if they never operated an airplane before, how can they complete the job? They can't. A person must learn. Knowledge is power. If we know little, then we can only do little. If we want to enjoy long lasting healthy relationships, we must do two things. First, we must carefully study the needs of our companions. And two, we must "study and learn everything we can about relationships." We now live in the information age. It's easy to gain access to good counselors and information. Educate yourself on romance, sex, and relationships.

How to Get Over a Break Up!

According to a sex bulletin article in a men's health magazine, twelve (12) is the number of times a month newlyweds have sex. Nine point six (9.6) is the number of times a month after six months of marriage.

Sixty-one percent of husbands report a decline in sexual satisfaction at six months. Forty-nine percent of wives report a decline in sexual satisfaction at six months.

Have you ever been "deeply" in love with a person but things didn't work out? Everything seemed so picture perfect in the beginning, but as time passed skeletons started to come out of the closet, secrets are exposed, and their true nature starts to surface. Deep down in your soul, your instincts tell you that it's not going to work, but you still remain optimistic. Eventually, you grow tired of fighting, cheating and arguing. Separation can be very painful, because we invest so much in our relationships. We invest our time, money, energy, our minds, bodies, and soul. Some people, because they are so stressed that they commit suicide. Others turn to drugs and alcohol as a way to cope with this difficult situation.

The first things I suggest is:

1. *Prayer*—You can talk to God, the creator, about everything. And you don't have to worry about HIM putting your business out in the street. Many strong men and women have overcome mental and physical trauma through the power of prayer.

2. *Family*—If mom and dad are still around, turn to them for love, support and comfort. Most parents have suffered from some kind of trauma in their lives. If your parents have not been

through a break up before, they know someone who has, so I'm sure they can provide some advice that will help you navigate through the situation.

3. *Positivity*—Occupy your mind and body with positive things like exercise. Exercise is very good because it relieves stress and it improves confidence, and now will be the time to lose the few pounds you have always wanted to lose. If you are alone in a big house or an apartment, consider adopting a pet. Maybe a dog or a cat can be good company. They will also be a responsibility.

I have been in many serious relationships and when they ended, I worked extra hours on my job as a means to cope with the heartache and pain that I suffered. When I finally got over the ordeal, my bank account was very, very nice.

I had to move back home with my mother because I needed to find myself. And I was financially unstable. Find positive ways to cope with the situation. Buy yourself some new clothes, shoes and go out and party in moderation. Surround yourself around positive people and go get counseling.

Improve Your Sex Life

Since the beginning of time, sex has been a very sensual, intimate, important part of human life, and culture. In the bible King Solomon had seven hundred wives and princesses, and three hundred concubines.

How was King Solomon able to sexually satisfy all seven hundred of his wives and princesses and concubines? Mind you, back then there was no Viagra. Solomon had to be in very good physical shape in order to maintain a strong mental relationship with all seven hundred wives and three hundred concubines. Solomon had to have a healthy diet, with a host of other creative things. Now I will share with you forty (40) steps to great sex. This article is by Victoria Zdrok, Ph.D.

1. *Hit the gym.* Physical exercise boosts levels of endorphins, the feel-good hormones, as well as testosterone, the hormone responsible for sexual desire and performance. Aim for at least 30 minutes of exercise three times a week.

2. *Give your love muscle a workout.* Pelvic exercises, also known as Kegels, improve ejaculatory control in men and enhance orgasms in men and women. Start by locating your PC muscle, which you use to stop and start the flow of urine. Then just squeeze as hard as you can and hold it for three to five seconds, release and relax for five seconds. This will have the most impact if you do a dozen or more repetitions, three or four times a day.

3. *Get some rays.* Moderate sun exposure puts you in the mood for

sex by causing your body to release the pleasure endorphins as well as the sex-drive hormone testosterone.

4. _Be a flirt._ Whether you're looking to meet women or are in a long-term relationship, flirting will undoubtedly enhance your sex life. Give her suggestive compliments. Casually touch her when you walk by, and give her long sultry looks. Flirting stimulates your sexual desires—and hers too!

5. _Try something new._ Alter something about yourself from time to time, whether it's how you dress or how you trim your beard, and vary your sexual script by trying new sexual positions and places and exploring new sexual techniques.

6. _Enjoy erotica._ When used in moderation, porn definitely enhances your sex life. But don't bring out your collection the minute you get her in your bedroom. Many women are not turned on by stereo typical male-oriented porn. She might prefer reading explicit romance novels together, or listening to erotic audio CD's or watching couple-oriented porn.

7. _Create the mood._ Eroticize your bedroom by putting in dimmer lights and investing in a nice, non-creaky mattress, satin sheets, lots of pillows and mirrors. Consider getting some useful props, such as the vibrator pillows. Turn off all electronic devices. Nothing kills the mood quicker than the sound of your

alarm clock or worse, your mother calling.

8. _Talk to her._ Communication is critical for healthy sexual intimacy. Listen to her sexual desires and tell her about yours. Engage in some active listening—as annoying as it sounds. The payback will be great sex.

9. _Make sex a priority._ Set a sex date, if necessary, because in our crazy, busy schedules, sex often gets put on a back burner. But also be spontaneous about sexual opportunities when they arise. Ask her to join you in the shower. Occasionally skip work or school and take a day-long sexcapade!

10. _Use good scents._ Certain aromas stimulate sexual desire. Essential oils, such as patchouli, sandalwood, ylang-ylang, vetirer, cinnamon, and vanilla, can increase sexual stimulation in men and women. And don't be afraid to work up a little sweat too. The pheromones in male perspiration stimulate sexual desire in women.

11. _Avoid sexual downers._ Aspartame (found in many diet foods and soft drinks), caffeine, and alcohol are vasoconstrictors. This means they work against blood flow, including in the genitals. Keep away from such rich foods as turkey, which will turn you into a lazy potato sack. Other common substances that may diminish sexual performance in men: aspirin,

antihistamines, over-the-counter cold, allergy or sinus medicines, potassium nitrate, lemon juice and vinegar.

12. *Enjoy foods that boost sexual desire.* Honey provides high sustained energy and peanuts increase testosterone levels. They can also be considered aphrodisiacs. Enjoy a peanut butter sandwich with some tea and honey! Because energy is important for good sex, eat high protein foods, such as fish, chicken, low fat dairy products, and beans.

13. *Take your vitamins.* There are natural nutrients your body needs for optimal sexual performance, such as omega-3s in conjunction with an Ester supplement, zinc, and vitamin D. These nutrients can aid circulation and overall wellness, leading to better sex. Vitamin E increases oxygen in your system. Your multivitamin also should contain iodine SOD. selenium, RNA, manganese, bromelain, cysteine, choline, and inositol. Consult a doctor to determine your optimal dosage.

14. *Review your options.* If you feel bored or turned off by sex, try sublimating your sexual energy by taking up a new hobby or finding a new passion in life. Or it may be time to make changes—whether it's finding a more suitable partner, starting an exercise routine, or seeing your physician, shrink, or sex coach.

15. *Get touchy-feely.* Physical touch is an immense turn-on for both of you. Hug her until she gets totally relaxed in your arms. Let her break contact. Give each other sensual massages.

16. *Lose the TV.* Studies have shown that couples who have a TV in the bedroom have half the amount of sex as couples who don't. Disconnect the cable and use the DVD player to watch erotica—preferably one you made with your honey.

17. *Go green.* There are numerous herbs and natural remedies that have been found to enhance libido, such as yohimbe bark, arugula, tribulus, damiana, ginseng, gingko biloba, kelp, balut, Borojo maca and of course, horny goat weed. But since different people may have different reactions, don't ingest any of these before you check with your doctor.

18. *Don't get smashed.* While a small amount of alcohol can cause you to have difficulty getting erections, and both men and women may have difficulty experiencing orgasm. Not to mention that while intoxicated you may end up having the sort of sex (Read: Unprotected) you will regret!

19. *Become a sexual explorer.* Have you always dreamed of having sex in a convertible, trying a three-some, or getting anal stimulation? Drop any embarrassment you may have about the fantasy and share it with her. It will encourage her to open up

as well and maybe even to try it out.

20. *Love yourself.* Masturbation is one of the best things for your mental and physical health. Pleasure yourself during sexual dry spells, because sexual prowess is akin to foreign language. If you don't use it, you lose it. Practice delaying orgasm by peaking and then allowing your erection to subside, which will allow you to last as long as you want during intercourse. Show your honey how you play with yourself—it will give her fresh new ideas on how to please you better.

21. *Take a walk on the wild side.* Try some bondage and discipline by tying her up and giving her a good spanking (then switching roles), or some domination and submission by having her give you orders on how best to sexually please her. Encourage her to go commando, and play with her discreetly in a restaurant or movie theater.

22. *Get your heart racing.* Research has shown that our brain does not discriminate fully between the adrenaline rush evoked by lust and that evoked by fear. Hit the roller coasters, go bungee jumping or watch a scary movie together.

23. *Groove to the music.* Dance is a major libido booster. Go clubbing or take ballroom dancing classes together. Encourage her to take belly dancing, stripping, or pole dancing classes. If

you're unattached, use dance lessons to meet women.

24. *Get an annual checkup.* High blood pressure, diabetes, thyroid problems, and other conditions can contribute to libido blues; so can their treatments. Discuss drug side effects with your doctor and request an alternative with minimal libido lowering effects, whenever possible.

25. *Just say no.* Marijuana and opiates may appear to increase libido, but they actually deaden nerve endings, decreasing our ability to get turned on and to feel orgasm in the long run. Take your pick—get stoned or get turned on!

26. *Rest.* Sleep deprivation is associated with lower libido, as well as with weight gain, irritability, and difficulty focusing. If you find yourself passing out into a deep sleep the moment you get her to bed, cut down on the java, skip the late show, and get enough much needed rest to have the stamina of a warhorse.

27. *Make yourself tasty.* What you eat can influence the taste and smell of your semen and even your sweat. In general, dairy products create the foulest tasting fluids, while meat and fish produce a fishlike taste. Garlic, onions, cabbage, broccoli, asparagus, and cauliflower make your semen taste bitter. To make your semen finger licking good, drink lots of water and eat lots of fruit (such as pineapple, watermelon, papaya, and

mango), as well as such vegetables, as tomatoes, carrots and cucumbers.

28. *Drop that excess baggage.* Being too heavy, especially around the mid-section, will decrease libido due to hormonal imbalances (fat stores estrogen, which reduces libido in men). Losing weight will also give you more confidence and allow you to try out new sexual positions. And remember, for every inch of stomach fat you lose, your penis will appear more prominent—the easiest way to achieve a bigger dick.

29. *Relax!* Stress is one of the biggest libido killers. Find a calm place, close your eyes, banish all thoughts, and repeat a mantra word, such as 'om.' Visualize a peaceful place, such as a beach or imagine yourself floating on a cloud. Then tense and release each one of your muscles, starting with your toes and ending with your face. Repeat the process until you feel like a yoga master—ready to take your lover on a tantric journey.

30. *Breathe deeply.* Put one hand on your chest and one on your stomach, then slowly inhale through your nose or through pursed lips to slow down the intake of breath. As you inhale, your stomach should expand. If your chest expands, focus on breathing with your diaphragm. Slowly exhale through pursed lips to regulate the release of air.

31. *Look on the bright side.* Optimists have better, more satisfying sex lives. So banish the habit of seeing the negative side of things. Don't internalize failures. For example, if you go soft during intercourse, don't think you're an impotent loser. Instead, realize that it happened because you were tired.

32. *Have a play-date.* They're called sex toys for a reason. They add playfulness and excitement to your life. They can also relieve performance anxiety by giving her multiple orgasms before you climax. Try toys for her, such as dildos and vibrators, and ones for you, such as cock rings and masturbators. Vibrating cock rings can deliver mutual pleasure, as can double sided strap-ons (don't knock 'em till you try 'em).

33. *Kiss off.* Kissing has numerous benefits from increasing saliva production, which improves your oral health to turning on you and your partner. Most women believe that if a guy cannot kiss, he cannot screw. So learn to be a master kisser. Start soft and don't ignore her face and body. For many women, kisses on the back of her neck, behind her ears, on her shoulders or even on her eyes can be as big a turn-on as a lip smacking smooch.

34. *See the dentist.* Poor dental health, such as gum disease, is correlated with erectile dysfunction. Bacteria produced by gum

disease can damage your cardiovascular system as well as your overall health and blood circulation.

35. *Check into a hot sheet hotel.* Get away from it all and pretend that you have just picked her up (or hired her services)—a great way to include a little role-playing.

36. *Talk dirty or send dirty text messages.* Leave her a phone message describing what you will do to her when she gets home, or send her a quick, lusty IM. Phone six is great foreplay.

37. *Explore her body.* Look for hidden hot spots, or moan zones, such as the line between her pelvic bones, or at the bottom of her buttock, or that ticklish spot behind her knee. Some people can orgasm from nipple stimulation, and a few even come from ear touching! Try dry humping, inter-femoral (closed thighs) sex, intermammary (boob) sex, or even armpit sex.

38. *Go tantric.* Assume such intercourse positions as side-by-side spoon to allow you to go for slow, leisurely lovemaking. Try the sweet torment of the tease, otherwise known as orgasm denial, as some sexual frustration enhances orgasm. Bring yourself and her close to orgasm and then back off, allowing for the buildup of sexual tension. Keep doing that as long as possible, winding up that spring of desire until it is ready to

explode.

39. *Don't skip the after play.* Orgasm triggers the release of oxytocin, the "warm and cuddly'" hormone that enhances closeness and intimacy. Take advantage of this oxytocin high by cuddling during those post orgasmic moments. For a woman, a good cuddle after sex really improves her satisfaction—and that will inevitably lead to her wanting more sex.

40. *Role-playing.* This is a sure way to spice up your sex life. If you're really adventuresome, let her play the male role!

CHAPTER 2 – The Reason Why Men & Women Cheat

Why do people cheat? First, we must analyze human nature and purpose. Our purpose on earth is to be in harmony with the CREATOR our HEAVENLY FATHER. And second, we must reproduce our DNA to have children, so we can repopulate the earth so the human race can continue its existence.

Generally, women look for one man who can satisfy all of her needs. On the other hand, men look for every woman to satisfy his one need.

A woman can be in a relationship with a successful businessman. He provides her with the best of everything in life, but if he fails to satisfy her sexually, there is a strong possibility that she might think about finding someone who can satisfy her needs. On the other hand, we have a guy who satisfies his woman sexually, but he is broke. And we all know that a woman don't want a broke man. I have personally witnessed it time and time again. Men are different. If we see a beautiful sexy woman we start to lust and lust when it is fully grown given birth to sin and eventually our lust will cause us to have sexual relations with other women.

In other words, if we see a sexy, beautiful woman and if we think that our spouse will not find out, most men will cheat. Talk to your partner. Find out what works and what don't work. Keep your relationship spicy by doing spontaneous things like role-playing or having sex outside in the rain. Give your spouse a full body massage.

I have learned that most women don't like men who are predictable. Don't be the kind of man who comes home from work, goes for the refrigerator, grabs a beer and watches the game. Sometime, surprise her with a gift or a trip to a place that she has been telling you that she wants to go to. Take her to dinner and a movie. Don't just exist. LIVE!

How do you know when you're in the right relationship?

People are like leaves on a tree when it comes to relationships. There will be people who will come into your life for a season, and there will be those who will come into your life for a lifetime. Many times we get the two mixed up. That's why our relationships fail. This is one way that we can tell the difference.

If your spouse's behavior is hindering the progression of the relationship, or if your spouse has a vice that makes you sick. And when you tell them that you dislike their behavior and that behavior is not healthy for the relationship, then if they try to change they are someone that's a leaf trying to grow into something greater. But if that person doesn't put forth any effort to change, then you should end that relationship.

But if your spouse is physically and mentally abusing you, get out of that relationship as quickly as possible, even if they say it will never happen again. If you have ever been in love before, you know that love is a very powerful addiction. When you love a person, it can be very difficult to let go. We invest a lot of time, money and energy in our relationships. As a result of these relationships, we might have kids together, a house, bank accounts and more. The fear of being alone and starting over can keep us trapped in an abusive relationship.

If you or someone you know are in an abusive relationship, be proactive and get help, counseling and any support you can get from family, friends and programs.

Are you or somebody you know in an abusive relationship? Do your spouse call you names when angry. Do they push or hit you? If so, what have you done? Do you love yourself? Would you hurt yourself? Then don't let anyone else hurt or abuse you.

Team Work and Team Effort

I sometimes look back at my past relationships and I have noticed that my girlfriend and I lack team work. It's very important to sit down and talk to each other about your long term and short term goals, and figure out creative ideas and ways to help both you and your spouse achieve your goals and dreams. Most people put forth very little effort in this area. There is no I in team. The key element in team work is the "we concept"!

When I was in boot camp some years ago, my drill sergeant always enforced *the we* concept. I hated *the we* concept at first because I didn't understand it. When one of the members of my platoon mess up, we all paid for it. Back then, I didn't realize that our drill sergeant was teaching us how to work together in difficult situations. My sergeant would say, "We are only strong as our weakest member." *The we* concept method caused us to think with creative ideas and help the weakest members overcome his mental and physical challenges in a positive way. The cliché "together we stand, divided we fall."

The Truth About People

Many times when we meet that special person, they often put on the mask of deception. They start out being very nice, kind and polite in the beginning, but when they become comfortable with you, the romance stops and their attitude becomes different. You might say to yourself, this is not the same person I fell in love with. We sometimes notice the change in their behavior three to six months after we have had sex with them, if we are lucky. Many times their behavior changes right after sex. It's important to take your time. You must do your homework and observe him or her very closely.

Oprah said on one of her shows, that when a person shows you who he is the first time, believe them. If he lies to you, then he is a liar. If she cheats on you, she is a cheater. We cannot change a person. We must find companions who share the same moral values that we ourselves believe in.

The 80 20 Rule

I believe that I can speak for most people when 1 say that humans are not perfect. Perfection is in the eye of the beholder. In my mind I can be perfect, but there would always be people who would dislike me because I appear to be so perfect.

I believe that if a person meets someone who meet 80% of his needs, wants, and expectations, he's a very lucky person. It is not wise to leave a person who meets 80% of your expectations, because they lack 20%, unless there is some abuse, or domestic violence issues.

If so get out of that relationship as soon as possible.

Sometimes we might leave a good person because they are a few pounds overweight. Thinking that the grass is greener on the other side, we end up with selfish irresponsible people. Now we realize that we made a terrible mistake, and what we have been looking for was right before our very eyes.

It's important to find a companion who shares the same morals, values and ethics as we do. To be equally yoked. To be able to agree on at least 80% of things. And 20% you may not agree with. It's common to have disagreements, different views on issues and arguments. Sometimes arguments and disagreements can be healthy for a relationship because it allows us to see the truth about ourselves. And we can vent. There are a lot of people who keep everything bottled up inside and that can be very stressful.

**

What is Love? How do I know if my spouse loves me? Love is defined by Webster's dictionary as Love is a noun. But love is a verb when someone says that he loves you. Love should compel him or her to do something. In the bible John 3:16 reads: *"That God so loved the world that he gave his only begotten son and whosoever believes in Him shall not perish, but shall have everlasting life"*

Love made God do something. He gave! When true love is present, love will treat ya right. Love will take care of you, love will nourish you. Love is polite, and love is not rude. Love is not selfish. Love is faithful. Love is honest. If you ever wonder does he or she love you, love should look like this.

In order to properly give love, we must first understand love. We must learn to balance love. What I mean is we must love our family as well as our spouse. And if a spouse tries to isolate you from your family, you should be very cautious of them. I would like to see young men protect their mother and sisters, make sure they get to work and school safely. I would also like to see young ladies obey your parents. Be wise and know you are worth. Know that you are a queen and act like one at all times. As fathers, brothers, and sons we must educate ourselves and our women. The energy that we gave is the energy that we will receive. The universal principle of reaping and sowing is very accurate.

In past relationships when I treated my woman kind and respectfully, with love, in return she treated me kind, respectfully and with love. But the moment I began acting foolishly she began acting foolish. I see it very often. A woman who's so deeply in love with a man. she is willing to do any and everything for him, but he is so blind that he can't see a good thing in front of his eyes. And likewise I have seen some ladies dog some good guys.

Love has many dimensions, and I would have to write a book about it. We are just covering a few dimensions.

Now, let's talk briefly about consciousness. Do you love yourself? How do you know? Seventy-five percent of the world is unconscious, comatose, and spiritually dead. Conscious or consciousness is being aware of the consequence of our actions. Love conscious is like being health conscious, self-conscious, and game conscious. How can you say that you love yourself when you continue to eat unhealthy foods, get very little exercise, or physical activity.

We pollute our environment with toxic chemicals. Are we aware of the fact that we are destroying ourselves and others? When we become love conscious, we protect ourselves, our environment and the people around us. We must first learn to honor and love the CREATOR. THE CREATOR has given us instructions on how to love, eat and live. We must awake and become aware of the destruction that we are causing on earth. Something is wrong when the younger generation is not outliving their parents. Parents, burying their children is at an all time high. Let's make a conscious effort to love ourselves. Let's love our children, love our environment, love our brothers and sisters. And love our "CREATOR."

CHAPTER 3 – Respect Her Mind

As a heterosexual man, I have encountered many beautiful, sexy, gorgeous women and all that I could think about was having sex with them. That kind of thinking and behavior has caused pain, stress, and confusion. My mind was so focused on the physical, I failed the most important part of the female body—the mind. Without the mental connection you have nothing.

Let's assume that you were in a serious relationship with a good looking person. One day you received a call that your spouse has been in a terrible car accident. Your spouse's face was badly injured. That beautiful face is now ugly. What would you do? Would you find another beautiful spouse? Or would you stay and help your spouse recover?

I know that this sounds like a cliché, but beauty, true beauty comes from within. And when two people have a mental connection, their relationship can weather the storm because they took the time to know each other.

As a young man I never really paid much attention to what my woman thought, her goals, or dreams. 1 just wanted some good sex. My woman would be talking and most of what she was talking about went in one ear and out the other. My old way of thinking undermined her ideas. To undermine anybody in this way is disrespectful. Women are not just one dimensional creatures. They have many dimensions and lair that's waiting to be explored and challenged.

But there are many women out there in the world who spend most of their time, money and energy trying to look good. These women are one dimensional.

The mind is the most powerful sexual organ of the body. Everything starts in the mind. Most pimps would agree that the mind is the most sexual organ. All of our fantasies play out in the mind. That's why it's so important to have that mental connection, not just sex but to know your partner. Be open to explore the depths of our most inner thoughts and ideas. Respecting her mind is to become conscious of our action and to seek understanding.

To meet on the intellectual level is to experience a greater, more quality relationship and a richer life. A small mind breeds bacteria. Having sex with an empty minded woman is like fucking a hole in the wall.

Food For Thought

Going into any relationship, we must take a few things in consideration. We must consider our spouse's health, financial status, mental condition, and self-esteem, religion and family. When entering in marriage we inherit our spouse's ills as well as their riches. Family is always our greatest riches. Even if they are a cruel, selfish, pain in the ass. If your spouse, who you love, has children from a previous relationship, we must receive them as our own. Their family and children become our family. We have to learn how to receive them and communicate with them. This can be a difficult adjustment in the beginning.

In the previous chapter I talk about listening to your spouse and then act on the things that are important to them if you are able. One of my friends and I had a conversation about our ladies. He told me a story. One day his lady wasn't feeling too good. They practically lived together and when she became sick he made her go back home with her mother. My friend filed to put forth an endeavor effort to help nurse his lady back to good health. I understand that he is not a doctor or medical physician, but his actions seemed kind of cold to me. My friend mentioned that he loved her.

We must be conscious that the measure of love that we give is the measure of love that we receive. And we must become conscious of what love is. True love would have made him move in such a way that he would have tried to do everything in his power to nurse her back to health. One of the biggest mistakes that my friend made was he didn't show his lady any love or affection. My lady friend went out searching for love and affection in other men. She didn't feel valued or appreciated.

My question is, how long has this neglect been going on? I didn't say a word to my friend. I didn't give any advice because I knew that he would have rejected it because of his level of maturity. I thought about my relationship and how I need to make sure my woman knows that I care dearly for her. I need to show her that I care about her health, her career, and our beautiful child.

Women look for one man who can satisfy all of her needs. And we think that it is hard work. But the irony of it is, we make it much harder than it really is. The problem with most relationships is we let the situations get so out of control, by the time we begin to repair it. It's either too late or almost too late.

Assume your wife or girlfriend and you just bought a new house, and a few months after you all moved in, your husband discovered that one of the pipes downstairs in the basement has a small leak that can easily be repaired. He continues to put off the repair of the pipes until several months have gone by and the problem has become worse. The small problem could have easily been fixed for about $20.00 or so. Now, the problem will cost a few hundred.

Early detection is the key. When you notice a small problem starting to develop in your relationship, fix it right away. Doctors tell their patients all the time that early detection is key to healing. Try to communicate and work out problems with each other. If that fails, seek help from counselors or someone who can help you.

When Is Sex Unhealthy by Dr. Jeff Gardere

Dr. Sigmund Freud, sex researchers Masters and Johnson and a bevy of behavioral scientists all agree that sex is a healthy and normal part of life. And why not? When sex is good, it can be very good. Heck, even when sex is lousy, it can still be pretty good. In fact, there are a myriad of reasons why Marvin Gaye was right; sexual healing is good for us. More and more studies are showing increased emotional and physical benefits from frequent safe sex, especially in marriage, according to About.com writers Sheri and Bob Stritof. These benefits include:

- Reduced risk of prostate cancer, heart disease and other illnesses

- Reduced depression and overall emotional wellness

- Increased level of commitment and a better emotional connection between spouses.

- Relief from menstrual cramps, general pain relief and less frequent colds and flu.

- Improved fitness level and help achieving weight loss (about 200 calories are burned during 30 minutes of active sex).

- A calming effect and relief from stress

Tracie is a 37-year-old software engineer who sometimes found herself completely stressed out by her very demanding job. But she also knew what she needed to do so as not to be consumed by the stress; have an all-out, no-holds-barred sex session with her husband Floyd, whom she affectionately referred to as her "relief pitcher." And believe me, he was happy and enthusiastic to help sexual healing. But there was an additional benefit to their great sex. It brought them closer together and strengthened the bond of their marriage. Yes, they were truly on the same team.

I am sure we all have some story in our lives about how sex has benefitted us physiologically and especially in our relationships. But wait—is sex always good for us and for our relationship? Sorry folks, and I know you hate to hear it, but the answer is no! There are obvious practices that can counter to health, such as sexual addictions, indiscriminate and unsafe sex with strangers, and, of course, infidelity.

However, there are more subtle sexual behaviors that we might unknowingly be practicing that can be bad for us and have a negative impact on our relationships.

Janice sought therapy after a number of failed relationships, or should I say relationships that failed to launch. Basically, as soon as she met a guy she was attracted to, she would jump in the sack with him. She had convinced herself that she wanted to experience these guys sexually, and that it was all about having fun and fulfilling her own needs. The problem was that she would grow to like her partners quickly and beyond just the sex, but they would move on and leave her emotionally stranded.

A few sessions of therapy got her to realize that many of her actions were tied to her being abandoned by her dad at a young age and being desperate to fill the void by any means necessary which, for her, meant sex. Therefore she became desperate to capture these men and would substitute sex for conversation and the natural process of just getting to know one another. Essentially, she was making sex the foundation of her relationship. And as men often do when women give it up too quickly, her partners were defining her as nothing more than a booty call and not the quality person that she is.

There are many other ways that sex can be bad for our relationship. They include:

Using Sex as a Weapon—Yes, sex can be used as leverage, and that's not a good thing. It's one thing to reward your partner for sex when he does something really nice, such as taking you to dinner, or even cleaning the house. But it's a horse of another color when you withhold sex out of anger to punish him. Sure, after some of his bad behavior you may not be in the mood, but you should discuss the problems instead of passive-aggressively withholding sex.

The same thing can be said for getting pregnant to capture or keep a man. In this case the fetus or child becomes the weapon. But in the long run this plan can become a ticking time bomb that hurts everyone involved. In most cases the father becomes resentful, the woman frustrated and the child is exposed to feuding parents.

Substituting Sex for True Intimacy—Sadly, this scenario plays out in too many bedrooms. We get into the lazy habit of thinking that sex equals intimacy. Well, it doesn't. Intimacy is not just a physical phenomenon; just as important is the emotional aspect, which requires effort on many levels. But sex substituted for intimacy is not just a lazy way to connect; it can also become a destructive way to shield one's true feelings. It's a lot like the O'Jays' hit song: *Your body's here with me, but your mind is on the other side of town.*

Unfortunately, too many people hide behind sex because they believe that if they put their feelings out there, they will get hurt.

Self-Medicating with Sex—Of course I endorse sexual healing in a committed relationship, but sometimes sex becomes a quick fix. Instead of trying to solve problems in our relationships through real communication and hard work, we turn to sex to soothe us. Sex then becomes a bandage on a wound that needs deeper treatment.

Using Sex to Fill a Void—In my practice I've found that one of the major issues we all share is how to handle being alone. Too often we just have to have the distraction of someone, anyone in our lives. As part of this thinking it seems very easy to fill that void with sex, indiscriminate sex, and even bad sex. This kind of behavior, if left unchecked, can be the beginning of a sexual addiction.

Summing Up—So what's my final love prescription when it comes to sex? Have it, enjoy it. Savor it and love it! Yes, it can bring you happiness, health and completeness. It truly has so many physical and emotional benefits, but if it is not bringing you closer to a true and healthy love of yourself and your relationship, in the words of another great singer Teddy Pendergrass, you may be headed for another love TKO. What you say about that?

A Moment of Abstinence

Recovery from any addiction or injuries require a period of abstinence. Like, for instance, if I was addicted to alcohol, and I decide to check into rehab, the number one rule of drug treatment is no drinking. Because if I don't stop drinking I would never be healed from my addiction. If I was a pro football player, and I injured my knee in a game, the doctor would recommend that I stay off my knee until it is healed. Likewise, after a bad breakup or a divorce you need to give yourself time to heal.

I sometime hear people say that the best way to get over a bad relationship is to get back into another one or the best way to get over a man is to find a new one. This kind of behavior is an act of desperation. And when we are hurting and our minds are not clear, we make the mistake of allowing the wrong people to enter into our lives, and we can find ourselves in a worse situation. When studying successful relationships, the couples who abstain from sex and focus on themselves for a while has a higher success rate.

One of the ways that I got over breakups is I focus on working and making money. I even had to move back home with my mom and save up my money. It was very embarrassing, but it was a good place to heal and refocus myself. The moment of abstinence is not forever.

It's only for a little while, to give yourself time to heal so that you won't bring all of the hurt and pain into your new relationship.

We must evaluate our morals, values and ethics that we seek in ourselves and in our spouses. There are many people who think that they need to be in a relationship. They are afraid to be by themselves and they sometimes tolerate abuse from their spouse. Being alone should allow us to love ourselves and to connect with the "CREATOR."

Self-Education & Life Experiences

There are a lot of good books and magazines that can offer some sound advice, and they can be very helpful in our everyday lives and relationships. You have to have a hunger to want to learn. Knowledge provides us with the tools to make the healthiest relationship possible. Education is the key to success. Education allows one to be free. Education teaches us how to properly read our spouse, and communicate on a mature and intelligent level. We must learn how to understand our spouse.

I have been in relationships and the women would often say, 'you just don't understand me.' And the frustrating part was that I really wanted to understand her feeling and emotions.

As I grow older I had to learn how to listen, and understand a few basic things about the female anatomy and how she communicates.

In general women communicate differently from men. We must pay attention to her body language and emotions. For instance, you and your spouse go out to dinner. You all walk past a clothing store and your lady notices a very beautiful dress in the window, but money is tight right now. You can't afford it. A few days have gone by and you notice that she is a little down and sad. So you ask her what's wrong honey and she answers nothing. But her body language and her emotions say different. The average guy would overlook her emotional signs and take her at her word. "Nothing is wrong."

The No Judgment Zone

The No Judgment Zone in the above title is referred to as our home, or place of business or any place that we might have control or a strong influence over. In the no judgment zone concept, we are not going to criticize each other for our faults or character defects, because we all have flaws, and we are all beautiful and special in our own way. We must realize that we can't change nobody. It's up to the person to change. They have to want to change and they must take the first step. When we care about a person, and they destroy themselves with drugs or alcohol or they might be lazy or unorganized, you might not want to be around them. When we judge a person we usually beat them down with our word. It makes our loved ones feel bad about themselves and make them angry.

The Five No's!

If your spouse, or the person of interest does not have "no morals, no values, no class, no charm, no God," that relationship will not last. God teaches us morals and values, and out of the five no's HE is the most important. HE alone is the CREATOR and sustainer of life. With HIM all the other attributes will fall in place.

Moral is the ability to judge right from wrong. Morals are principles that you will not compromise. For instance, having sex with your spouse, cousin or having sex with one of your spouse's best friends, would be morally wrong if you don't share the same morals. Some couples have an open relationship, and they might not care who their spouse has sex with as long as they know who it's with. The immoral mind is lawless and selfish, thinking of only self, with no regard for others, and the feelings and needs of others.

The immoral person can be evil, spreading their wickedness around to others like cancer. And you can forget about them telling you the truth.

Values are things that we value, like family, children, home, careers, and education. We should value God, and our lives. It's important to have values because they give us a sense of direction.

A person with no class is usually wild and behaves ignorantly. You can't take a person with no class anywhere because they will act like a fool, and embarrass you. I love a classy woman. A classy woman carries herself honorably and she is respected everywhere she goes.

To all my dear beloved sisters all around the world, I love you all. You all are man's most greatest resource next to GOD ALL MIGHTY ALL POWERFUL. Please start behaving honorably. Yu are the first teachers of the child, and the whole community is watching you all.

Gift Lovers & People Lovers, Knowing the Difference

We all have gifts given to us by the CREATOR. Most people are not conscious of "gift lovers," because they can be deceiving. We all are gift lovers and there is nothing wrong with it. The problem is when we think people love us, what they love is our gift. Have you ever wondered that when we have large amounts of money, we have many friends. But when our funds have declined, our so-called friends declined as well. Likewise, when we are successful in business, sports, music or profession we seem to have many extra friends and associates. Some of these associates are gift lovers.

One day I was watching music videos, and Beyonce Knowels videos came on. I said to myself, *"Damn I love that woman. Her beautiful voice, amazing body and killer dance moves had me in love."* But the truth is I was in love with her gifts—the gift of her beauty, the gift of her amazing voice and her killer dance moves.

People lovers take the time to get to know you. They learn about our strengths and weaknesses. They know our likes and dislikes. They know our favorite foods. People lovers, after they get to know us they make a choice to love us for who we are.

CHAPTER 4 – Money Management & Finances

Over 60% of marriages and relationships end due to mismanagement of funds and/or a lack of money. In most cases a lack of money really is a curse. Couples who are financially stable have the resources and freedom to do the things that they enjoy doing. Money is a tool. Now I would like to direct your attention to an article from Black Enterprise magazine

Principle. I will ensure that my entire family adheres to sensible money management principles. Steve and Pamela Cromity possess all the trappings of upper-middle-class comfort. They own a home in Lansdowne, Pennsylvania; a time-share in Kissimmee, Florida; and employ a nanny to care for their son and daughter, Steve III, 12, and Christina, 10. For the Cromity's the key to the good life isn't the couple's annual $150,000 income, although it certainly helps. The entire family avoids impulse purchases, they say. And when they do buy something, they bargain shop. What separates Steve, Pamela, and their children from most Americans of any economic level is a strict adherence to proper money management. The Cromity's make every effort to never pay full price for anything. Last October, for instance, Steve paid $100 for a refurbished iPhone, when the retail price was $399. For Pamela's birthday in September, he bought her a pre-owned iPhone from AT&T for only $50. And when the couple wanted to upgrade from a 32-inch to a 50-inch flat-screen television, they decided not to pay full price or use credit to buy it. It took a year and a half before they found a TV they wanted at a price they were willing to pay. In the end, they spent $750 for a $1,100 television. "I believe in delayed gratification. You don't get things that you want automatically. You wait until the time is right," says Steve, 43, a staff architect and business development manager who earns $72,000 a year plus bonuses. "Everything that we get seems sweeter because we get it at a discount."

Steven and Pamela apply the same approach to debt. "We have a substantial income but we still have to be conscious of every dollar, because we know it's very easy to get ahead of yourself," says Steve, who pays more than the minimum payment each month on his debt.

After Pamela received an M.B.A. in 1990 and Steve got an M.A. in 1993, they owed $70,000 in student loans. They have paid off all but $1,000. They plan to be rid of all debt, including their mortgage and home equity loan, in 15 years. The Cromity's are teaching their children to enjoy the finer things in life while not paying top dollar. "We want to always have plenty, but we still want our children to know what it is to sacrifice," says Steve. They also want the children to live graciously and give generously, says Pamela, 43, a Senior Pharmaceutical sales representative who brings home $67,000 plus

$10,000 in bonuses.

So far, Steve III and Christina are following their parents lead. They each get $5 a week for allowance and bonuses of up to $20 per activity when they excel in academics or sports. Instead of spending his money on video games or clothing, Steve III saves it. Over the last year he has put away more than $300. "That is a significant amount of money for someone this age." says his father. "He buys one thing that he really wants, but he will always reserve a considerable amount of cash. He will even ask what chores he can do around the house to earn more money," says Steve.

Even at the age of ten, Christina also understands the value of thrift. She keeps a cache of coupons for clothing stores and avoids paying full price, just like her father. "I think my children know that there is a time when they can get the things they want because they've saved. They've been frugal, and they made an effort," says Steve. "They've learned to make whatever dollars they have go further."

The notion of giving to others also plays an important role in how the Cromity's raise their children. Since 1990, Steve and Pamela have helped to fund scholarships that enhance cultural diversity at their alma mater, Pennsylvania State University. The couple also thinks it's important that their children see them give money in church every week.

The Cromitv's Advice

- *Talk about money.* Children learn money habits from their parents. Talk to them about the money decisions you make and why you make them. "My kids see how my wife and I are a team. We don't just do things off-the-cuff," says Steve. "We communicate with each other constantly about money." The jump start coalition for Personal Financial Literacy (www.jumpstartcoalition.org) is a great place to go for resources that will help your children learn more about money management.

- *Teach your children how to budget.* Spending can be a thrill, but being broke is downright depressing. Teach your children how to manage their income and cash outlays. "We want them to learn now so that later on when they get older and they have to do it on their own, it is not as difficult," says Pamela. "Show children how rewarding it is to stay within their financial boundaries and not to accrue debt. While grocery shopping, make lists and set a financial limit," says Pamela. "Have the children help you try to stay below that limit. Make budgeting fun by purchasing a financial game. The board game Moneywise Kids (www.talicor.com $20) teaches children how money works as well as how to make and manage a household budget.

- *Show children how to be charitable.* Let your children accompany you as you do volunteer work, and show them the financial statement confirming donations you have made. "It's important that they see me giving whenever possible in whatever form it takes," says Steve. "Also, put them in the practice of giving. Don't allow your children to accumulate things or be wasteful," Steve advises. "Teach them to donate to charity. Toys and clothes that they have outgrown."

The 10 Wealth for Life Principles:

1. I will live within my means.

2. I will maximize my income potential through education and training.

3. 1 will effectively manage my budget, credit, debt, and tax obligations.

4. I will save at least 10% of my income.

5. 1 will use homeownership as a foundation for building wealth.

6. I will devise an investment plan for my retirement needs and children's education.

7. I will ensure that my entire family adheres to sensible money management principles.

8. 1 will support the creation and growth of minority-owned businesses.

9. I will guarantee my wealth is passed on to future generations through proper insurance and estate planning.

10. I will strengthen my community through philanthropy.

Chemistry One on One

When two people have chemistry they work well together. They click because they are on the same page. When two human beings have chemistry they have something to work with, something of substance. I'm not talking about the blue is my favorite color stuff. I'm talking about the big guns, like what kind of book are you reading? How do you treat your mother? Do you have any children? How much time do you spend with them?

We must have chemistry on a deep intellectual level. Do we share the same religious belief? And does he or she know the value of the dollar. Have you ever met someone, who was very attractive and maybe he or she don't have a lot in common with you? You all have different moral and values. Different goals and views about health and life. But despite of all your differences you hook up anyway. After just a few months or years down the line, things just are not working out for you all. And your spouse began to look less and less attractive to you. The physical attraction is the most shallow component of a relationship.

Chemistry is the ability to connect on an intellectual level. To be able to call your friend up on the phone and talk for hours and not get bored. Without chemistry on an intellectual level, we really don't have much to work with. We should look for chemistry on many different levels as well, like moral values, religion and more. How can two walk together unless they both agree.

The Three Riches

Riches come in many forms, shapes and sizes. The most common or important is family and money. Money is necessary for the buying and purchase of goods. In today's society the wealthy have excess to better education, health care, food and housing and more. People who are financially stable are less stressed, and they are usually well respected among their family and friends.

Riches or money also bring about confidence and prestige among friends. Money allows a person to experience a kind of freedom. You can travel to all the places your heart desires, and money can change lives. A person can have all the material things in life and still be unhappy.

A person can be in a room full of people and still feel lonely. People with money must be cautious of the people they have around them because, with money comes fake friends—people who have hidden agendas.

I grew up poor, but I have a big family. My family and I always found a way to laugh and have fun. The happiness and joy that I experience with my family is priceless. The joy that I experience when I had my daughter Rokyah, made me feel like I had won the lottery for a million dollars. Having children is one of our many purposes in life, passing on our DNA from generation to generation, watching a child grow and learn and develop into a man or woman is amazing. Children can also be a real pain in the ass, as well. They can cause many heartaches and disappointments if they are disobedient. Sometimes the trials and tribulations in life might make you want to give up, but we sometime think of our children, what will happen to them if we give up. The responsibility reminds us that we must hang in there. The third riches in life is in direct relationship with the "CREATOR" of all things. Through a careful investigation of things and praying for the truth, we will find "HIM." And when we find "HIM" it will be so rewarding. And when HE begins to speak to you, you will experience a peace and a joy like never before. And if you obey HIM you will live in peace and harmony. The greatest riches of all is the "CREATOR." HE will give you the knowledge, wisdom and peace to enjoy all of our earthly material possession.

CHAPTER 5 – Physical & Mental Separation

Separation can be very hard for most of us, especially when we are in love. Being away from your spouse for a few days can be healthy for your relationship. The time apart gives us a chance to miss and appreciate our spouse. And when they come home, the lovemaking is usually good.

When I think about mental separation, a picture of an elderly couple who sits around at home on the sofa, watching TV all day and doesn't say too much of anything to each other, come to mind. A lack of communication is the first sign of mental separation. When we are unable to express ourselves properly through intelligent dialect, we begin to do one of three things.

1. We shut down and stop communicating.

2. We become aggressive and force ourselves, our views and ideas on others.

3. We give up and run from the relationship.

Listening is another component of mental separation. When we stop listening to our loved ones, the relationship is in trouble. How is listening a component of mental separation? When a person stops listening, they usually are not paying you any attention. And if they are not paying you any attention, they usually have their mind focused on other things. And when we cannot be attentive and focusing our minds on our loved ones, we are now mentally separated.

Selfishness is the active force behind this separation. At times we became so selfish that we will not compromise, and meet our spouse in the middle. We can sometimes become so focused on our dreams and our goals that we neglect our loved ones, which is selfish. We must learn to pay attention to our loved one, get to be pro-active of their goals, dreams, thoughts and ideas. As men we must listen to our women.

If your lady has had a hard day at the office and when she comes home from work and she tells you that her feet hurt, run her some nice hot bath water, and give her a foot massage. Learn to listen and then act. If your spouse is pursuing a career in music, comedy, or acting, be supportive and help them succeed. Help educate them on the business side of their career. It's a known fact that most women are so caught up in their spouse's life and career, these women sometimes put off their dreams, goals and career. They are busy with the children and the household or they sacrifice everything for the development of their spouse's career.

Listen & Act

Let's assume we have a young couple who just married. The husband owns a barber shop. The young wife decides to open a small clothing store. After a few months of opening the businesses, they both are doing fairly well.

Early one morning the wife opens the clothing store and discovered that someone broke into the store. She calls her husband and informs him of the situation. Meanwhile the husband has just gotten a new business proposal. He has a business meeting with his new partners. The husband tells his wife, "Honey I need you to get ready for the meeting, and wear that little blue dress." He tells his wife after this deal we will have enough money to buy a yacht.

I know that this story sounds strange, but this kind of thing happens all the time. Sometimes we get so caught up in our own goals and dreams/careers that we neglect our spouse's goals and career. In the above story when the wife informs her husband that her store was broken into, he should have stopped what he was doing and assist the emotional needs of his wife. As men, we sometimes don't understand the emotional needs of our women. We must learn how to listen and act. The women in our life—whether it's our wife, mother, sister or daughter—will tell us the things that they need or the things that we need to do for them.

Women must listen and act upon the things that are important to the men in their life also. We can improve our relationship if we apply this simple method. If your spouse says, "Baby, you have been going out to the club every day this week. I really want to spend some time with you. Let's have a few drinks, cook dinner and watch a couple of movies and relax." Do it for her.

Men, we must allow our women to be free. Don't treat her like a prisoner and you are the prison guard. That kind of behavior will only cause her to pursue other things. Be her friend and partner. Men, we must be responsible and have a clear vision of the direction of our family.

Let's become better listeners. If we will learn to listen, it is one of the master keys of virtues. It will take you down a road of success in life and after you listen, you have to do something.

Progression

What sense does it make to be in a relationship that's not progressing? You're right. It makes no sense at all. Our goals and dreams in life should be to improve our conditions whether it be spiritually, mentally, physically, or financially.

Why are so many people in relationships that are not moving forward in the above categories? For most of us, finances are the most important, because our survival depends on it. Our food, clothing, housing, health care and education is associated with money. In our relationship we should be working together and saving our money.

You know the old cliché—if you don't work, you don't eat. Why would you want to be in a relationship with a person who is not trying to work or educate his or herself. But if your spouse is taking care of the children and the household, that is work and it can be a hard and stressful task.

Like money, knowledge is power. It's just as important as money. In the book of Proverbs, a fool and his money will soon perish. A foolish person will allow someone to trick him out of his possession. I have wasted time and money in dead-end relationships that displayed no signs of progression. A relationship were two ignorant people with no sense of self or direction. I hope that I can share some of my knowledge with you and you learn to listen and act.

We should be moving forward and progressing in every area of our life. If you work at "McDonald's" and your spouse works at "Walgreen's," you and your spouse rely on public transportation to go back and forth to work. But if you and your spouse own a car, you will save time and money. It will be in the couple's best interest to make a conscious effort to save their money together, and buy a dependable used car. If the couple saved about $2,500 and they purchased a car. Each month, after they pay the bills, they have about $300 extra for the car. In eight months they save $2,400.

As partners in a relationship, we should learn how to put our minds and money together to make progress. If we put our minds and money together we can achieve our goals and dreams much faster. This method is not hard. It is a common sense approach. Remember to pray and use good judgment. If your partner will not work with you, ask yourself is this the right relationship for me?

Mint Condition

Mint condition is usually associated with cars. You might hear someone say. I'm selling a 1987 Chevy and it's in mint condition. If an old car is in mint condition the owner must have taken good care of it. The owner of the car must constantly repair anything on the car that needs fixing. He must change the oil and transmission fluids. He must get the car washed and waxed, and a long list of other things.

In our relationships, we must keep them in mint condition. If you want your relationship to stay in mint condition, you have to tune it up regularly. As human beings our needs change regularly. The things that I needed when I was 19 years old may not be the things that I need when I'm 25. We must continue to explore the emotions and needs of our loved ones. Our goals and dreams change. Our thoughts and ideas change, and so our needs change.

Many times in relationships and marriages, we think that the person we committed to is the same person we committed to 25 years ago. In order to keep the relationship in mint condition, your spouse and you should travel together, learn together, and experience new things together. Keep your sex life spicy by trying new positions, but never bring new sex partners into the relationship. There are many ways to keep the relationship "like new." But it's hard work.

It has been said that the key to staying in love is to fall in love over and over again. Make sure that your partner knows that you love and appreciate them. Sex is a very important element of a relationship. Some people might say that sex don't matter, but the urge to have sex can be so strong that we can be burning with the desire to have sex and not to mention the human existence depends on it.

In order to have a great sex life we must become comfortable together. And you must communicate with your spouse. Find out what does it for them, so that they can achieve the maximum orgasms. Build your spouse's self-esteem. Tell them that they are intelligent, beautiful and if they have a good sense of humor, tell them. Help them improve in the areas of their lives that they are the weakest.

Albert John Murphy

CHAPTER 6 – Spiritual & Universal Laws

Have you ever been attracted to a person who you know was married, or in a committed relationship with someone else? Have you ever seen a married person or a person who you know who was in an committed relationship cheating on his or her spouse? Let me warn you. It is never a good idea to have an affair with a married person or a person you know that's in a committed relationship. The end result is always bad, because there are universal laws of moral and when you break them you automatically subject yourself to judgment.

The CREATOR has given us these laws so that we can live in harmony and peace with each other. In the bible, the Old Testament, the CREATOR gives Moses "THE TEN COMMANDMENTS" to give to the "children of Israel." HIS purpose for giving the commandment was to instill peace and order among the children of Israel so that all the other nations would see the human knowledge and great wisdom of THE CREATOR. The people were living like animals at that time. They were killing their children and having sex with anybody they pleased.

The Ten Commandments are not a religion. It is good laws for instance: They shall not commit adultery. Let's assume you're having an affair with a married woman and her husband caught you in the act.

There is no "telling" what he might do to you. We can assume that he would be so angry and jealous, that he starts attacking you. There have been millions of people that have lost their lives prematurely because he or she got caught in adultery or cheating. YAHWEH THE CREATOR said it best they shall not commit adultery. I have heard pastors and preachers say that people won't keep the commandments because of our nature to rebel. We must learn to exercise self-control. When we see a beautiful person, sometime the urge to make out with them can be so strong that we burn with the desire. The problem is when we cannot control our emotions and desires, when we lose control of our emotions, we cannot make conscious decisions to uphold our moral responsibility to protect ourselves and others.

Marriage

If a woman finds a man who she cares for, and if she values marriage, when she finally gets married she will feel stable, confident and complete. She will also feel secure. Marriage is a holy covenant made by the CREATOR with a male and female.

Women usually value marriage a little more than men; especially if she is 35 years old or older. She most definitely would be willing to settle down. Women value marriage more than men, because having relations is a bigger investment for a woman because if she becomes pregnant she has to carry the baby around in her belly for nine months. Her body will undergo mental and physical stress and her emotions will be running wild, not to mention the pain she will endure giving birth. The reason why women are so willing to get married is they don't want to give birth to a child alone. And she doesn't want to raise a child alone. Women who want to get married are smart and if they wait to have sex until she is married, she will be extremely valued by her husband.

Why are men so afraid to get married? Most men who are afraid to get married probably have been hurt in the past, or they have seen someone close to them betrayed in marriage. The fear of being married to a perpetrator is not worth the risk. And it is much easier to pass through life with no wedding ring attached. Sometimes we commit to people that we think we know, and then find out that they are another person. As men, we have been told that the married life is boring. Another reason why most men don't want to get married is because some women give up the pussy too soon. If she gives it up to me on the first date, how' many other men have she done it with. Men love sleeping with women on the first date, but most will not commit to them. Ladies if you made that mistake before in the past it's cool. Just don't make that mistake anymore. We all have made mistakes before, especially in relationships, but the irony of it is we must learn from them.

My brothers and sisters, the TEN COMMANDMENTS given to us by our HEAVENLY FATHER YAHWEH. Anybody who keeps the commandments is very wise and intelligent. The commandments are "ten" intellectual keys to living a healthy life. It is not a religion, but a way of life. In order to live a long healthy life, our whole lifestyle must be healthy.

For example, if I eat right and exercise but I'm having unprotected sex with ten different women, and the ten women are having sex with other men, there is a good chance that I might contract a sexually transmitted disease. This is a classic case of living an unhealthy lifestyle or a person can eat right, exercise and not get enough sleep. And if a person is not getting enough sleep, eight hours to be exact, can be unhealthy. A person can eat right, exercise and get the proper amount of sleeps but he or she can be a thief. Stealing is a very bad moral act. And if someone caught you stealing their stuff, they might give you a beat down. Stealing is not a healthy way of life. When two people are living a "whole healthy lifestyle" it would be easy to enjoy the fruits of a healthy relationship.

The Ten Commandments is a tin plate for success.

1. *I am the Lord your God YAHWEH, who brought you out of the land of Egypt, out of the house of bondage. You shall have no other gods before ME.* You might think that this commandment is not important, but it is. One might say "What does it have to do with a healthy relationship?" When we put others gods before the CREATOR, they hinder us from having joy and

peace. There are two forces in this world GOD—YAHWEH, and the devil. Good and evil. There is no middle ground. There is no neutral. If you are not serving God YAHWEH, then you are serving the devil. GOD YAHWEH is our strength. If HE brought the children of Israel out of slavery, then "HE" can, and will bring us out of our bondage.

2. *You shall not make for yourself a carved image. Any likeness of anything that is in heaven above, or that is in the earth beneath, or that is in the water under the earth. You shall not bow down to them nor serve them. For I the Lord your GOD YAHWEH am a jealous God visiting the iniquity of the father upon the children to the third and fourth generation of those who hate "ME" but showing mercy to thousands for those who love Me and keep my commandments.*

Now first let's break this commandment down into two parts. First, the CREATOR warns us not to make any strange idols for ourselves and don't worship them. Back then in Moses era, the Egyptians made demonic images out of stone, wood and gold. They believed that the demonic lifeless idols they made were Gods. They prayed to the images and worshipped them. Many other tribes of people made Gods out of wood and stone and worshipped them as well. History repeats its self. Many people are still worshipping idols made out of wood and stone to this day.

In some churches they worship idols made out of wood and stone. This is an error and it causes the people to be confused and weak. In times of tribulation when the people pray to these lifeless idols, nothing happens.

Now the second part of this commandment is when the CREATOR said, "I am a jealous God visiting the iniquity of the fathers upon the children to the third and fourth generation. HE is talking about generational curses. The reason why "some" relationships are cursed and our children suffer is because we have not kept the laws and the commandments of our CREATOR. These laws and commandments are designed and put in place so that all humanity can be in perfect harmony with each other. And when we failed to keep them, everything and everybody is out of harmony. When we don't keep the commandments we become inhuman. When we go around and have sex with any and everybody and killing each other, we are like animals, not human.

3. Thou shall not use the Lord God YAHWEH's name in vain for the Lord thy God will not hold him guiltless that take HIS NAME in vain.

What this commandment means is don't square falsely by HIS

NAME.

4. *Remember the Sabbath day and keep it holy. Six days you shall labor and do all your work, but the seventh day is the Sabbath of the Lord your God YAHWEH. In it you shall do no work: you nor your sons, nor your daughter, nor your male servant, nor your female servants, nor your cattle, nor your stranger who is within your gates. For in six days the Lord YAHWEH made the heavens and the earth the sea and all that is in them and rested on the seventh day. Therefore the Lord YAHWEH blessed the Sabbath day and hallowed it.*

What this commandment means is every Saturday stop doing your weekly work. Rest and remember, and worship our CREATOR. Remember the Mercy and Love and all the blessings that the CREATOR has done for you and your family. Many people have said that this commandment is not important. They say things like, "It does not matter what day we serve God on. Every day should be holy." But the CREATOR knows that we can't keep every day Holy. We are going to make mistakes in life.

With time, knowledge, patience, and studying HIS laws, commandments and statutes we can become the children of YAHWEH. The objective of the Sabbath day is for all of God Yahweh's children to rest from all of our weekly jobs, chores and activities and spend time with HIM and focus on our relationship.

The Ten Commandments are broken down into two parts. The first four commandments teach us to love, honor and obey the CREATOR. And to be in harmony with the CREATOR. The second part of the commandment is the last six commandments. They teach us to love and respect other human beings—brothers and sisters. And treat them the way that we would like to be loved, respected and treated.

5. *Honor your father and your mother, that your days may be long upon the land which the Lord YAHWEH is giving you.*

My father was addicted to drugs and alcohol. Even though he struggled with the many demons of his addiction, he demonstrated his love every day. He was no saint, but I can say that he instilled morals, values and ethics in me at a young age. I can remember him telling me to honor my mother and father, that my days be long upon the land. Everything that my dear mother told me was always true. Every time I failed to listen to my father and mother's words, I end up in some kind of trouble.

6. *You shall not murder.*

7. *You shall not commit adultery.*

Is this commandment taken from a religion? No. it is a good law established to keep peace and harmony in the midst of us. Could harmony exist in the midst of us if you commit adultery? No, there would be problems. This does not represent a religion; it is a good law. If you caught some one having sex with your wife or woman, you are not going to think about religion. You will think the offender has violated that law. It does not make a difference whether you are a Baptist, Methodist, Hebrew, etc. The God of Creation works by formulas. He works by an order, even if you do not understand the order. The order does not change. If you do not know the order, the order still does not change. Someone may say that they did not know it was forbidden to commit adultery. But they should have known! And if I catch you, whether you know the order or not, is not going to change what I may do to you! Not knowing is no justification.

8. *You shall not steal.*

9. *You shall not bear false witness against your neighbors.*

10. *You shall not covet your neighbor's house.*

You shall not covet your neighbor's wife, nor his male servants, nor his female servants, nor his ox, nor his donkey, nor anything that is your neighbors. Covet as defined by

Webster Dictionary states covet: vb desire enviously. It's shameful to witness folks disliking other people because they want the things that other people possess. We see this happening every day. A modern term for covet is haters. A hater is a person who hates you because you have more money or material things than they have. A hater will hate you because you have a nice car, lots of money and a beautiful woman. They might dislike you because you work hard on your job and you hustle odd jobs on the side to make extra money to buy nice things. The commandments are not a religion. They are divine law given to us by GOD ALMIGHTY YAHWEH to govern us so that we can have peace and harmony among each other. It would be heaven on earth.

Love Consciousness

Love consciousness is knowing what love is and the affect that true love has on our lives. Love is taking action. Love should compel us to do something. Love also should have boundaries to protect each other; for example, our children. We must teach them right from wrong so that they will have conscious minds. If I bring my child outside to play, and she comes very close to the street and I tell her to stay away from the streets, she laughs and comes running toward me, but five minutes later, she ran back toward the street. This time I give her a little spanking to let her know that the streets are dangerous, and that daddy means business. When a parent loves his child, we must correct and teach them right from wrong. Please don't abuse your child. When we teach and correct them we develop our children's consciousness human mind. Consciousness is being aware of our actions, whether they are good or bad. When a person is conscious, he or she is aware of their actions, and the consequence of those actions. There are people in this world who are unconscious. They think that they can do anything, and it will have no effect on their life. Some of us think that we can go around having sex with anybody we please and it will not affect us. But many people have lost their lives, and are hurting because they behaved in this kind of activity. We pollute our environment and communities by building nuclear plantations that burn toxic chemicals in our air. Some of these toxic chemicals cause cancer, breathing problems and a host of health risks.

Temptation

When a man or woman starts a serious relationship or marriage, we are more tempted than usual. If you are a man in a committed relationship, women are drawn to you. Some of her friends might even want some of the magic stick. Likewise, some men are drawn to women that are in relationships or married. Some of your spouse's friends might flirt with her a little, and if she flirts back she might, let's just say, you know the rest.

We all are faced with temptation on a daily basis. You might see a person who's extremely attractive, but we must ask ourselves, is it worth it? In most cases it's not worth it. If you are happy and you love your spouse it's not worth it. We invest too much time, money. Money®, love and energy and did I mention, money in our relationships. Many marriages and relationships have been destroyed from infidelity. After we weigh our options and if it's not worth it, don't do it. Think about how your spouse will feel if you get caught cheating. And think of the heartache and pain you will feel if your spouse cheated on you. Pray and ask the CREATOR to help because we all fall short at times.

Doubts

Doubt, as defined by Webster Dictionary read as follows: Doubt-vb 1: be uncertain about 2: mistrust 3: consider unlikely n: uncertainty 2: mistrust 3: inclination not to believe.

Most of us enter into relationships with mistrust, and we should be cautious when we first become involved with a new person. We must test the water before jumping in. "Trust is earned through time and communication." Trust is like a seed. It starts off small, then it either grows and blossoms or it dies. However, if you have been in a relationship for six months or a year, and you still don't trust him or her. then you might have a problem. Whenever doubt outweighs the love, the relationship will not grow to its full potential. In relationships that don't have any trust, it can be easy to give up, and walk away from the relationship.

For instance, you have an old car that's not so dependable. Sometimes it starts and sometimes it won't. You grow tired of dumping money in it. Your worst fear is one day you might get stuck some place. You have doubts about the car, and decided to sell or junk the car. The irony of this is let's say, that you have an old car that gave you no problems and the car is dependable. You will not be in a hurry to sell the car. In any relationship we look for people who we can trust and will have our back. A person might ask his or herself the question: Can I count on her or him when things get really tough? The number of couples whose marriage or relationship end over financial problems, are very high. But doubt is the creative intellect behind the split.

Let's say that your wife loves to shop. Everything that she sees, she buys. She spends to the point that you all are almost bankrupt. She spent all of your life savings that you worked so hard for. You doubt that you will see a good future together, so you tell her, I think that we should get a divorce.

Bringing Out the Best in People

How do I bring out the best in the people that I love and lead? We must be careful not to manipulate the people we love, but let's try to motivate them. The difference is that you are a manipulator when you try to persuade people to do something that is not in their best interest but is in yours. You are a motivator when you find goals that will be good for both sides, and then form a high-achieving high-morals partnership to achieve them.

Throughout history we can find the best motivators. Wellington reportedly said that when "Napoleon was on the field, it was in balance, the equivalent of fighting against another 40,000 men."

Phil Jackson led the Chicago Bulls into six championships and when he left the Chicago Bulls he led the L.A. Lakers to many championships. Phil Jackson was able to get that extra effort from his players, that extra ten percent. If Phil gets a ten percent extra effort from fifteen players, it will equal out to be one-hundred fifty percent extra efforts. And that equals championships.

If a motivator wants to get that extra effort, whether it's a parent, school teacher or football coach, we have to expect the best from the people we are leading or trying to motivate.

Doctor Alan Loy McGinnis, author of "Bringing Out the Best in People" teaches 12 rules on how to bring out the best in people. You must read Doctor Alan Loy Mcginnis' book.

Rule Number One: *Expect the best from the people we lead.* Chicago Public schools are cursed with under expectation of the students. Some teachers say that the students are lazy and don't want to learn. This kind of attitude hold a negative effect over the students, and the classroom. Expecting the best out of a person requires a certain level of faith. You are telling them that I believe in you, you can do it. In the movie "Pretty Women" Julia Roberts played a prostitute and the middle-aged wealthy businessman doesn't treat her like a prostitute. He treats her like a lady and eventually she began to live up to his expectations. Executives of large companies say that it's hard to find good help nowadays. We have the power to call out the worse in people, or the best in people by our expectations. This happens all the time. We sometimes accuse our spouses of cheating and many times they are not. When we accuse them of cheating, what we are really saying is "I expect you to cheat. I don't trust you." And our expectations can cause them to cheat. What we should be saying is "Hey honey I love you and I want you to know that I appreciate you and thank you for being honest and faithful to me!"

Psychologist C. Knight Aldrich, who worked for years with delinquent children, wrote a fascinating article some time ago in a psychology journal, explaining how parents can quickly turn their children into thieves. Here's the way to do it.

Let us say that your son, as most children do at some time or another, engages in some petty theft. Perhaps he steals a package of candy. If you say to him, "Now we know what you are—you're a thief. We'll be watching you from now on," it is quite likely that he will steal more and can quickly graduate from stealing candy to stealing cars. On the other hand, you can react with both firmness and gentleness by saying, "Tom, that wasn't like you at all. We'll have to go back to the store and clear this up, but we're not going to make a huge thing of it. What you did was wrong. You know it was wrong and we're sure you won't do it again." After such treatment most kids' stealing careers are over. The principle is very old; by assuming a negative attitude and reflecting back to people all the data about faults and their behavior becomes worse. By assuming a positive attitude and concentrating on their strong aspects, you put them in contact with their good attributes and their behavior becomes better. A careful study of the people we hope to motivate has two benefits. In the first place we can gather data with which to build our motivational appeal, and in the second place, we pay people a great compliment by devoting so much energy to knowing them.

Have you ever wondered why some marriages were successful and others weren't. The marriages that are successful, the couples seem to be experiencing pure ecstasy. I ask myself, what's the secret to their happiness. A careful investigation on this subject. I have found that one of the most important ecstasies consistently reported over the centuries is the breakthrough of knowledge discovering the solution to a problem or bursting into some new field of learning. In the Old Testament when describing the sexual experience, it mostly uses the verb "to know." When we are told that "Abraham knew Sarah" it is an eloquent and apt description of sexual love, which is both a very deep penetration and a very complete engulfing. In marriages where ecstasy is preserved, the man and the woman never stopped seeking to know one another. They do not assume that because they have been married for twenty years they know what the other is thinking.

Let's pretend that you just came home from work and your son is on the living room floor unconscious. You quickly call the paramedics. They take him to the hospital. The doctors don't ask any questions. They inject your son with medication and then take him right into surgery. I know that my example sounds extreme. It would be very foolish on the doctor's part for not asking any questions. What if the little boy has an allergic reaction to the medication?

A friend of mine complained about his girlfriend not having a job or going to school. She just sits around the house all day doing nothing. He would often complain, and say things like he is tired of her laziness. Like so many of us, my friend made an assumption that she was lazy. He never took time to find out why she didn't want to work, or go to school. Had my friend carefully studied her needs and not assume she was lazy, he would have found that her parents instilled in her that a man should take care of his woman, and the woman should stay at home and not work. Had he known his girlfriend's needs, he could have formed a tailor made plan for her to motivate herself and help her figure out what she wanted to do in life.

Rule Number Two. Learn and study the needs of the people close to you. The best way to motivate the people we lead is to study their needs and design a plan that best appeals to those needs.

Dr. Alan Loy McGinnis says that the best way to bring out the best in people is to treat them in a positive, encouraging manner. Capitalize on their gifts and begin with their present needs and desires.

Dr. Alan McGinnis wrote, "I know an art teacher who rotates among five different schools each week, which means that she works for five different principals. They all have different leadership styles, she says. One woman, for instance, dresses very elegantly and administers her organization with a certain amount of aloofness. She is totally professional and the school moves ahead smoothly.

Another principal also has a good school, but he is much more informal. A hail-fellow-well met type, he is loose and friendly and likes to take playground duty just for association with the kids. "But do you know what school has the morale?" this teacher asked. "It's the one where the principal tries hardest to be popular with everyone. He'll say things to us teachers like, "Don't bother to come to the school program tonight if it's not convenient. I know you have a long drive." Maybe he thinks the way to succeed with people is to be easy on them, but it backfires. Everybody on that staff is trying to get transferred. Such a laissez-faire attitude conveys the message. This school is not worth caring about. It is the same reason that the easy teacher and the sloppy boss are never respected—they obviously do not care either about excellence or about persons. And although we may have squirmed under hard teachers, we usually look back with gratitude to their determination that we use our potential.

If we are going to enforce high standards, it will require us to tell people when they do not meet those standards. In their book, "The One Minute Manager," Kenneth Blanchard and Spencer Johnson advocate giving "one-minute reprimands." One of the surest signs of a weak manager or a poor parent is the fear of telling people in your organization when they have erred. Here are some simple suggestions for handing out a reprimand:

1. Do it immediately

2. Before going further, confirm the fact. Be sure your information is correct.

3. Be very specific in telling them what is wrong. Try to criticize their behavior, not their motives.

4. Show your feelings, anger, annoyance, frustration. We must be honest and straightforward when the people we lead do not meet our standards.

We have to make sure that our standards are not too high and not too low, but in balance. For instance if our children get all "F's" on their report cards, tell them that you expect them to get all C's on the next report card.

Rule Number Three. Create a foundation for excellence. Failure as defined by Webster Dictionary states n. 1 absence of expected action or performance, 2 bankruptcy, 3 deficiency, 4 one that has failed.

I believe that we all have experienced failure in one form or another. A man who fails and gets back up and tries again, he is like gold going through the fire to be purified.

I experienced failure early in life. When I first learned to ride my bicycle I fell off that thing about a thousand times. But I kept trying until I learned how to ride.

Comedian radio host, and author Steve Harvey has been married three different times.

He said that it took for him to fail a few times in his marriage in order to finally get it right. He has been able to capitalize from his failure. Steve Harvey wrote a book called "Act Like a Lady and Think Like a Man." Now he is a New York Time best seller. Some CEO's and managers have a very low tolerance for failure. If an employee fails, he might lose his job. People who fail are usually determined to succeed because nobody wants to be a failure. An employee who fails has learned what not to do. They can be our most valuable asset.

I met a man on the street who was one step away from being homeless.

He once had everything; a nice apartment, cars and all the women wanted him. He had money and prestige and respect among his peers. He said if he had a chance to do everything over, he would do things differently. But he said that he learned from his mistakes. The best managers expect their people to make mistakes, and instead of replacing staff constantly, they recognize that it is more efficient to teach people how to cope with their failures and learn from their mistakes. In other words, they are not so much judge and disciplinarians as they are coaches and teachers, and they know that when people fail, it is one of the most important intersections for their motivational work.

Dr. Alan Loy McGinnis says that the one thing that teachers and educators discuss when they get together is how do we build inner drive in our students. I remember when I was a young boy in grade school my teachers had a hard time motivating me. And to be honest, my teachers didn't put forth much effort in motivating us. I was mostly interested in music and business.

Had my teachers understood the principles of using the student's dreams and goals to achieve better grades. Most teachers and educators spend very little time in asking their students about their goals and dreams. Some years ago I started to get very deep in my faith and religion. I was so overzealous that I wanted everybody I came in contact with to be saved. I would encourage the mother of my child to take an active role inside the church. I couldn't motivate her into taking an active role in the church because she didn't want to do it. It was not her dream, or goal or desires. The best way to motivate a person is to ask them their goals, dreams and desires, and then form a high moral, high achieving plan to help them achieve their goals.

There was a famous singer from the U.K. His parents put him through medical school.

He didn't want to be a doctor. His real passion was music. He told his parents that he was going to leave school to pursue his music career and that if he is not successful in one year, he was going back to medical school. His parents supported his music career. His music career flourished and he became a big success. Have you ever wondered why some artists fail and other succeed? In order to succeed in anything in life we need a strong support system.

Sometimes we need someone to cheer for us when nobody knows our name. We need someone to laugh at our jokes, and tell us that we are funny. There is no better support system than family. We need someone to jump on the bandwagon before we put wheels on it.

Rule Number Four. If they are going in the direction that you want them to go, encourage them.

Late one night, August 2010, I was witching behind the music of lil' Wayne, a young rapper, whose father was not a part of his life. His mother remarried and his stepfather, whom he cared dearly for, was murdered. Growing up on the drug infested streets of New Orleans, all odds was against Wayne. Wayne developed his rap skills at the age of twelve. He was signed to cash money records. Lil' Wayne has faced many trials and tribulations along the way. He has proved himself to be one of the greatest rappers in hip hop. In 2008 Weezy's Tha Carter 111 was released and shut down the game scanning 1.5 million units in its first week. The album won several awards including a Grammy for best rap album. While he was on top, Weezy used his status to bring awareness to his own label, Young Money Entertainment which featured acts like Nicki Minaj and Drake.

After watching lil' Wayne's success story, I was very motivated and I began to think of ways to develop my publishing and writing career.

Rule Number Five. Find people who have succeeded in the dreams and goals that you have and follow their methods.

For many years coaches, religious leaders, and politicians have used this principle. Basketball coaches use Michael Jordan as a model to encourage players to try their hardest, and to win games. Christian leaders and pastors use Jesus and his teachings to encourage believers to live righteously. Muslims leaders use the prophet Mohamed. And Hebrew Israelite use Moses.

The truth of the matter is we are all influenced by someone, whether it be a family member or the guy next door.

Parents or family members can be so quick to recognize and point out our failures, faults or bad behaviors, and overlook our accomplishments We should use every opportunity we can to celebrate the achievement of the people under us whether an employee or friend, or family members. The art of complimenting produce confidence, and self-esteem and morale in the people we love. The art of compliments is positive reinforcement.

My older brother, Bobby, is an expert in positive reinforcement. When someone in our family or a friend starts a new job or has a wild and crazy idea, we can always count on Bobby to support and encourage us. This is my first book that I have written. When I first started writing this book, I would talk about it with family members and friends and some of them laughed and thought that I was joking. But not Bobby. He told me that it was a good idea and he ordered me a publishing guide. And he told all of our family members and friends that I was writing a book. And he spoke with such faith. As a beginning writer I really needed encouragement. That, Bobby gave me. It really motivated me.

The power of positive compliments can be found to be effective in babies. When a child takes his first steps and the parent cheers them on by clapping and laughing, the child senses that he or she is doing something right and the child would be highly motivated to take more steps. Some people say that it is possible to overdo compliments until it becomes meaningless. This is as bad as giving too much criticism and reprimands. Let's say that you are teaching your dog to sit. Every time he follows the command and sits, he gets a doggy treat. But once the habit has been established, the doggy treats should become a little massage on the head. Parents and bosses need to remember the principle of shaping. Once good habits are established it is harmful to compliment a person all the time.

We have been discussing the art of compliments and its effectiveness. It will be morally wrong for me not to mention that we must praise the CREATOR of the universe when we praise our beautiful, wonderful, loving CREATOR. He makes our lives worth living and richer and meaningful.

Rule Number Six. Use positive compliments to encourage people to succeed.

We talked about the power in positive compliments, which is very effective. As human beings we also need negative truths. Pastor and political leader, James Meeks, has one of the biggest churches in Chicago. Managing the morals and values of thousands of people, one might ask what is the key to his success? Why are thousands of people flocking to his mega church every week? With a congregation so big he would scold them with the truth and warn them of the consequences of sin. He would use personal stories, biblical stories to illustrate the ill effects of a sinful lifestyle. He also used positive reinforcement to encourage his congregation. He built a trust relationship with them. They are like his family.

Rule Number 7. Use both, positive compliments and negative truths to balance relationships.

Most parents consciously or unconsciously use this rule all the time. For instance, if a child is playing with an electrical outlet, you will have to scold them promptly enough that the behavior could change on the spot. And repetitiously using this scold/reinstruction method, the behavior pattern changed. The parent was out to shape habits. "Some are kissing mothers and some are scolding mothers, but it is love just the same and most mothers kiss and scold together," by Pearl S. Buck.

We all have the spirit to achieve and to do great things. It can be used as an effective motivating force. The competitive instinct. The irony of it is it can be a destructive vice.

Women often compete with each other. They sometimes try to out dress the other women at church or at work. This competitiveness can be destructive. A few years ago I attended a bible study class, and the minister warned us not to compare ourselves too high or too low. A friend of mine says that everything is a competition. He said that he tried to walk better than the next person, exercised harder than the next person, and he tried to read more books than everybody. He said the day when we stop competing, other people will pass us by. My friend also said when we stop competing we get comfortable. There's always somebody who wants what we have. They want our woman, money, cars and our homes. Dr. Alan McGinnis, in his book "Bring Out the Best in People," tells a story about Charles Schwab, who supervised all of Andrew Carnegie's steel mills, had a mill manager whose men were not producing their quota of work. "I've coaxed, pushed them. I've threatened them with damnation and being fired," the manager told Schwab. "But nothing worked. They just won't produce." It was the end of the day and just as the day shift was leaving and the night shift was coming on "Give me a piece of chalk," Schwab said. Then turning to the nearest man he asked, "How many heats did your shift make today? Six." Without another word Schwab chalked a big figure six on the floor and walked away. When the night shift came in, they saw the six and asked what it meant. "The big boss was in here today." the day man said, "and he chalked on the floor the number of heats we made." The next morning Schwab walked through the mill again. The night shift had rubbed out six and replaced it with a big seven. When the day shift reported for work the next morning they saw the big seven chalked on the floor. So the night shift thought they were better than the day shift, did they? Well, they would show them a thing or two. The men pitched in with enthusiasm and when they quit that night they left behind them an enormous, swaggering ten. Things were stepping up. Shortly, this mill, which had been lagging way behind in production, was turning out more work than any other mill in the industry. And what was the principle? Here is Schwab's description of it: "Sometimes the way to get things done is to stimulate competition. I do not mean in a sordid, money getting way but in the desire to excel."

Rule Number 8. Use healthy competition to achieve goals.

Jesus YAHSHUA the Messiah, when he was running low on motivation he would go somewhere by himself and pray to God the Heavenly FATHER ALMIGHTY YAHWEH.

CHAPTER 7 - Meet Me Halfway

In a serious relationship we have to meet each other halfway. If your spouse is not willing to compromise at some point in the relationship, the relationship will eventually fail. Please, if your spouse is trying to get you to do something illegal, or morally and spiritually wrong, then by no means compromise. The mother of my child hates it when I ask her to do something for me, like print something off the internet, and I ask somebody else to print the same document.

One day I was having a conversation with her and she began to tell me how upset it made her when I did that. I was not conscious that it made her so mad. I honestly didn't think that it was a big deal. She felt like I didn't trust her enough to take care of the business. And because it made her upset, I apologized and promised that I wouldn't do it again. I know that it might sound like a small issue, but it is very serious because it is a trust issue. If we can't trust each other, our relationship is nothing. The first problem that comes your way will ruin the relationship. It's like building a house on sand. When a good storm comes, it will blow the house down.

Ruined Beyond Repair

When the integrity of a relationship is ruined there is nothing we can do, but learn the lessons from the relationship and move on. But there are many people who try and save a ruined relationship. I'm always optimistic that there is hope. The problem is life is short. We don't have a whole lot of time to wait for a selfish spouse to change. Some people are just not ready to settle down at the same time that we may be ready to settle down. Some young people plan to settle down when they are forty or fifty years old.

Let's assume we have a young man who is educated and he hasn't had a lot of experience with females and relationships. One day he meets an attractive female who's older and more experienced in this area. After a few months the relationship gets serious and they decide to live together. The woman knows that the young man is green, so she take advantage of the situation. She is very flirtatious toward other men and she stays out until three or four o'clock in the morning. She lies to him and tells him that she was out late with her girlfriends clubbing. The truth is she was out with another guy. After several months of her lies and cheating, the young man finds out. The couple fights and argues about the situation. She apologizes and tells him that it will never happen again. But she continues to find new and clever ways to lie and cheat. She tells her girlfriends that she is not ready to give up her love affair.

Every since the young man found out his girlfriend has been cheating, he does not trust her anymore. Whenever she leaves the house he constantly calls her phone and asks her her whereabouts. And he tries to make her stay in the house as much as possible. Could this relationship be restored? Or is it ruined beyond repair?

It's obvious that the young man does not trust his girlfriend anymore. The young man is under a lot of mental stress. His lack of trust is causing him stress and the stress is causing him to behave like a prison guard, rather than her boyfriend or companion. He's keeping his girlfriend locked in the house makes her feel like a prisoner. They're playing the wrong positions. When we play the wrong position, the relationship will not progress. It will only become more difficult to handle. If the couple in this story wants their relationship to work, they must forgive each other and rebuild the trust. If this has happened to you, you understand that it's not easy to trust that person again. You will always have that thought in the back of your mind. "I wonder if he or she is cheating on me." Remember that we cannot change our spouses because we are not "God." We can only try and help them. It's up to the individual to change. Helping them means giving our loved ones the proper tools they need in order to succeed. It's very important to understand and remember our position in a relationship. I can't be my wife's husband and her father. I can only be her husband. If I try to be her father, it will make the relationship very, very difficult to manage.

Toxic Relationships

Arguing, fighting and cussing are some of the usual signs of toxic relationships. In some toxic relationships the couple don't know "who they are" because they don't know how to spend time by themselves. Before we get married we should learn to take ourselves out on a date. See do you find yourself interesting and exciting. Focus on your strengths and weaknesses, and form a plan to improve in those areas. People in toxic relationships fail to communicate properly and effectively. We have all witnessed the fighting and yelling and the name calling, people who were once in love poisoned by the ills of life. Children watching their families fall apart. Some of these children receive no counseling and they grow up thinking that abusing their spouse is normal. This toxic "mind set" is destroying families all around the world.

Women who are victims of domestic violence stay in the relationship because they have seen their mothers being abused or someone in their families being abused. The killing part about this is that they think that they are in love. Don't get it twisted. Women abuse men too. Most women abusers do so on an intellectual level. They use and manipulate kind hearted, loving men. Some people call these women "man eaters." And then there are also men who abuse mentally. Some people stay in a toxic relationship for so long until they grow toxic. If they don't heal from the toxic "mind set" they will ruin future relationships.

And they might not know why their future relationships are failing. The toxic mind set can also affect their ability to parent. We have to be very careful of the things we let our children see, and the way we treat them. A child's mind is like a sponge, absorbing information, attributes and characteristics. If you or someone you know is in an abusive relationship, talk to them about getting help. Help them, and be supportive through the healing process. Talk to a counselor, pastor, preacher, and tell them that you need some help. Prayer is a powerful tool that can help us overcome many things in life. Sometimes the toxic person can make us so weak that we do not have the strength to leave. Fear of looking like a fool. The fear of being homeless, careless, or moneyless because we have become dependent on an over abusive spouse. The embarrassment of moving back home with your parents. Prayer to the ALMIGHTY GOD of Creation is what we need.

The Ideal Couple

When I think about a healthy relationship, I ask myself the question of who has set a positive example for our country to see? A relationship that displays honor, trust, commitment, faithfulness, dignity and grace. The beauty of two intelligent beings coming together and working hard to achieve each other's goals. A relationship that will build confidence in our children and create opportunities for the betterment of their future, and provide them with resources that will improve their health, safety and education. A relationship that displays an authentic and genuine love. A love that shines in the shadow of darkness. A love like this the whole world can see. When thinking of an ideal couple, who would be better candidates than Barack Obama, the President of the United States and first lady of the United States. Michelle Obama.

The first lady and the president have shown such a love and commitment to each other, the United States and around the world. They have also shown great courage. They are both under a great deal of pressure of being a positive role model for their families and community. They truly are role models for the world and they are handling it with such grace and dignity. They are examples that brains triumph over bronze. That love triumphs over hate. That education triumphs over ignorance and healthy living over sickness.

Now, let's look deeper inside the life of the Obama's. Michelle Obama and her mother gave a personal interview on how Michelle Obama's mother, Marian Robinson, raised her and her brother and Mrs. Robinson taught them how to use common sense and how to think.

ESSENCE: "Mrs. Obama, what does being the first lady mean to you?"

MRS. OBAMA: "It's an honor and a privilege when you walk into the White House—at least automatically felt a level of obligation. This is a big responsibility, a wonderful platform and I just want to make sure I take every advantage to serve as a role model, to provide good messages, to be a supportive mate to the President and to make sure that my girls are solid."

ESSENCE: "What has been the most difficult part of this transition?"

MRS. OBAMA: "You know I would have to say that the transition has not been that bad at all. Having my mom has made all the difference in the world. And our friends and family have been with us every step of the way, so we don't feel alone at all. And what I have said to people before, I am most surprised by the fact that we probably have had more normalcy over this last month as a family than we've had in years. So now we have a place where we are going to be for a while. We eat dinner as a family. We spend way more time together than we have in years and it really feels good."

ESSENCE: "Mrs. Robinson, how has it felt to see your daughter step into this historic role?"

MRS. ROBINSON: "Well, to me it's overwhelming. I never doubted that she could do this. She is doing it with such grace and dignity. So I am just proud."

ESSENCE: "And what do you hope to see your daughter achieve as America's first lady?"

MRS. ROBINSON: "I just hope she does what she wants to do. (chuckles) Because the things that she wants to do are very important.

They mean a lot to her."

ESSENCE: "Mrs. Obama, you spoke at length on the campaign trail about women achieving a work life balance. Do you plan to continue that conversation in your role?"

MRS. OBAMA: "Absolutely. The reason the conversation came up during the course of the campaign is really just a manifestation of my life, and of what all the women that I know are grappling with. When you have children and a career or a job and you're trying to make it all work, it's tough. Women and families, we need to have truthful and honest conversation about what it requires to do all that we ask of families and women."

ESSENCE: "And how do you find balance in your life right now?"

MRS. OBAMA: "Unlike most women, I have a lot of resources. I have my mother living with me. The White House has a staff of people who are there to make my life easy. I don't have a full time job, although I work very hard in the role of First Lady. But I have a lot of resources, so I have been able to achieve the balance because I have the support I need."

ESSENCE: "Mrs. Robinson, what is the one thing that you have learned about your daughter through this process that perhaps you didn't know before?"

MRS. ROBINSON: "Michelle has always been Michelle. And she has always accomplished whatever it was she set out to accomplish. I have always looked up to Michelle because she has been able to do things that I couldn't do emotionally, psychologically or physically. I think she is amazing."

ESSENCE: "Mrs. Robinson, what do you think your late husband, Fraser Robinson III, would say about this moment?"

MRS. ROBINSON: "You would not be able to shut him up! He would not be able to stand this. He would be beaming until you would just want him to stop talking. He bragged about Michelle and her brother, Craig, before they had even done anything. He always encouraged them, and when talking about Craig and Michelle, you could just see a smile on his face, whether it was there or not. He just enjoyed these two people."

MRS. OBAMA: "I always felt that my father and my mother were unconditionally rooting for me. And kids need that. Looking back, that played such a huge role in building confidence in me and my brother very early. Whether we succeeded or failed, we had two people who lifted us up and supported us. There was never anything that I could imagine that I would need that they wouldn't bend over backwards to make sure that we had. There is just a sense of security that allows you to take risks. People think that it comes from wealth or generations of access and success, but it doesn't. The security of your parents' love really gives, you the foundation to think that you can fly. And then do."

ESSENCE: "Mrs. Obama, write Alice Walker wrote: 'If women of the world were comfortable, this would be a comfortable world.' Queen Rania Al Abdullah of Jordan has said, 'As you educate a woman, you educate the family. If you educate the girls, you educate the future.' "What do you think you can do as First Lady to advance the interests of girls and women around the world?"

MRS. OBAMA: "The thing that I have the most control over is serving as an example of what's possible when women from the very beginning of their lives are loved by the people around them, particularly the men in their lives, because I was surrounded by a father and brother and uncles and grandfather who cherished me and loved me. It doesn't have anything to do with money. It has everything to do with just fundamentals of life. So I also want to do a lot of talking and connecting. And then there are also things we can do as a society. We can look differently at policies that affect women and families, such as pay equity, which is something that Barack has already addressed. But that is just the beginning. We have to talk about flex hours and exercise and nutrition and health and what that means. And we have to talk about values and about our relationship with men. All of those are part of the conversation that I think we need to have, not just in this country but around the world." (Editor's note: President

Obama recently created the White House council on women and girls. It will be chaired by Senior Advisor Valerie Jarrett, who was profiled in our April 2004 issue).

ESSENCE: "Mrs. Obama, you and the president like to get involved in the community in which you live. You have already begun to do that, getting out to visit local agencies, schools and Howard University. Have you identified other issues that you would like to explore in the Washington D.C. area?"

MRS. OBAMA: "We want to look at nutrition and health. I still want to focus on military families. I also want to make sure that the kids in this community get access to the White House. Barack and I feel that we occupy the White House as temporary guests. This is the people's house. We want to make sure that kids who have never seen the inside of this house and have never seen the opportunities that come from life—whether it's listening to a concert or hearing a scholar talk about an issue or seeing all the wonderful examples of the people who work here and make this place run—I want to make sure the kids in this community know what is right in their midst. So, as important as it will be for me to get out, it is just as important to have the community come here. We are going to be doing a lot more of that in the years to come."

ESSENCE: "One of the most important issues that Washington, D.C. is tackling is HIV, and for African-American women it's devastating cases identified between 2001 and 2006 showed that among women who tested positive for HIV, nine out of ten were black. Do you have any thoughts on how you, as an African American woman with a background in health care, can make an impact?"

MRS. OBAMA: "We must talk about testing and education and information. When we were in Kenya, Barack and I took an AIDS test publicly because that is part of reducing the stigma associated with the disease. Truthfully, I think the answers to a lot of the issues come from self-esteem. Young girls and women have to believe that they are worth something more. They have to see opportunities for themselves beyond a relationship or beyond what's right there in front of them. That's what makes young girls make the decision to demand that for their future. But if you don't give young girls that vision and the confidence to postpone all of the immediate gratification, all the education and testing in the world won't change how they feel about themselves."

ESSENCE: "Mrs. Obama, how has your mother influenced your own development as a mother?"

MRS. OBAMA: "It's endless. It is not just influence—she made me who I am. She completely underestimates her role in who I am. She always says, 'You came here that way. I just stayed out of your way.' That's not how I saw it. My mom is an incredibly intelligent and insightful person about life in general. From the time we could talk,

94

she talked to us endlessly about any and everything with a level of openness and fearlessness that made us believe that we were bright enough to engage with an adult, that we were worthy enough to ask questions and to get really serious answers—and she did it with a level of humor. There were many times when we were in the midst of getting spanked or disciplined and she would start cracking up. She taught my brother and me not to take things so seriously; to work hard but to learn to laugh at situations and laugh at yourself and then to move through it. So many of the lessons that I learned from my mom and my dad around the kitchen table in our little bitty apartment are spinning around in my head every single minute of my life."

ESSENCE: "Mrs. Robinson, is there anything you would like to say to African-American parents about how to raise their children?"

MRS. ROBINSON: "My sisters and I always called our children 'little people.' I think when you do that, instead of saying they are babies, you look at them as a little person, growing up to be an adult. I just think African-American, and I am sure most people everywhere, do not realize how much kids absorb. You can start very, very early because they are listening. They love conversation and soak up information. The main thing that I think needs to be taught to children is the ability to think and make decisions. You don't have to have a lot of information, but you have to know how to get through the process. If you make mistakes you don't (just) decide I will never do that again.

Think through it. Figure out how it came out the way it did." MRS. OBAMA: "You think the decisions have to be grand ones like what college are you going to and whether you are going to do drugs, but it starts when you are four, making the decisions about what you are going to wear."

MRS. ROBINSON: "… what time you go to bed."

MRS. OBAMA: "This was our life growing up. So when it was time to go to college and make decisions about our courses, and our friends and dealing with teachers and situations, we had all of this practice. We had deep conversations when we were five and seven and eight because we would get into real serious debates. And it wouldn't just be 'no.' It would be, 'well, no let's think about that,' and then it was like, 'how, we got to think about it and now talk about it.'"

MRS. ROBINSON: "When my son would have to make a decision he didn't want to make, he would say, 'Aren't parents supposed to tell their children what to do?' I was like, 'No you decide.' "

MRS. OBAMA: "But it takes time. I think that ultimately that is something that we have to realize as parents now. Because having a child is a huge investment. The minute they are here you are full and until the day you die. It (requires) a lot of mental and emotional persistent that my parents always had. There was never a moment that they were not parenting. There was never a time when they just kicked up their feet and said, 'You are on your own.' Now (my mother) says that—but it never happened. There was always some active kind of engagement, discussion and explanation about it that helped us put it all into perspective, even when we were young. I see that in my girls now. They are very capable of making some really interesting decisions because of conversations we had when they were three and four. You see it already at seven and then it's like, you were listening!"

ESSENCE: "Mrs. Robinson and Mrs. Obama Essence readers tell us that they believe the sight of three generations of black women living in the White House can have a transformational effect on the negative and stereotypical image of black women beamed around the world via cable, music videos and reality television. Do you believe this is true?"

MRS. ROBINSON: "I believe (we make) a nice picture, but it's not necessary. It was the tradition in most families where you had generations (living together) and most of it because economically it worked out better."

MRS. OBAMA: "For me (our image) is a reminder of what is already the reality. The women in videos and the stereotypes are just not the truth of who we are as a community. We already know that because we are living these lives every single day. It's nice to have this reminder in the White House, but I would say we don't need it. But sometimes in the black community those stereotypes define us.

Sometimes we start internalizing something that is not even true, so (maybe our family) can be a reminder that all you need to do is look around your own community and you will see this same family in churches and in schools."

MRS. ROBINSON: "And then you have—for economic reasons—grandmothers nowadays have to work. So you don't want the grandmother to feel like they're less because their grandmother is not around."

MRS. OBAMA: "This is one model of what a black family can look like, but there are hundreds of others that work just as well. And again, we know this because these are the lines that we have had. Whether it is three generations or two or some mixture—maybe it's a father and daughter. We also don't want to get too stuck on one model. The truth is the black community is strong and full of smart, gifted and amazing men and women and we know this. Maybe the Obama's and Robinson's help to reinforce that, but we are reinforcing a reality that has been there all the time."

ESSENCE: "Mrs. Robinson, you have so much great advice. Have you thought about writing a parenting book?"

MRS. OBAMA: "We are working on it." (laugh)

ESSENCE: "Black women have some of the highest rates of volunteerism in the country, and it is something that was emphasized on the campaign trail. In what ways would you like to see African Americans engage in order to improve their communities and by extension, the country?"

MRS. OBAMA: "I would echo what Barack would say time and time again. Individual responsibility is the first step. We all have complete control over the decisions and choices we make in our life with our own families, whether it's turning off the TV and making sure that your kids have some structure and do their homework. Whether it's making sure that you cut your lawn and pick up the garbage in front of your house. If we are all tending to our gardens, that will strengthen the black community, first and foremost.

If we are volunteering in our kids classrooms. Even if we are being hit by this economic downturn, we can take the time that we have and invest it in our schools and our communities or work in our churches. Now is the time that we need everybody rolling up their sleeves and finding a way to add value to their families and their communities."

MRS. ROBINSON: "Maybe we just need more emphasis on education for young people. We need to expect more out of them because it's in there. We don't ask for it. We don't insist. Years ago the poorest of poor people insisted that you get your education. My theory is you can get a good enough education to get a job at a bad school, but you've got to at least attend it.

Then if you are attending a school that you don't think is so great, then do something about making it great."

ESSENCE: "Mrs. Obama, what is your Mother's Day wish for your mother and black women?"

MRS. OBAMA: "I want her to be as happy in her life as I am in mine. And she probably says the same thing about me, but I want her to enjoy the fruits of her labor, because she has laid a foundation that to me gives her the right to sit back and enjoy."

ESSENCE: "Mrs. Robinson, are you enjoying all this?"

MRS. ROBINSON: "I really am. You want to know why? Because my children are good parents. It makes it very easy to be a grandmother when your children are good parents."

MRS. OBAMA: "There isn't a relationship in a family that is more important than the relationship a child has with her mother, or someone in that role, and we have to value that. We cannot wait to value it. We've got to value it each and every day. I just wish for all the mothers and children out there that they take the time to reach out, to forgive, to love, to share, to embrace, because nothing in your life will ever be more important."

The reason why I put this article in my book is because when I was reading this article I agreed with the First Lady and her mother, Mrs.

Robinson. I hang on to her every word.

The First Lady discusses some very important issues concerning women's health, education, morals, values and confidence. Mrs. Obama stressed the need to teach our young daughters and girls how to see a vision for their lives. A vision that will lead them into good health and success. A vision to see beyond the stereotypes and myths associated with the women and young girls in the African-American communities and all around the world.

A vision to become great parents, who have the common sense and wisdom to raise children that will be healthy, positive men and women who will make a conscious contribution to our communities and to our nation, and all humanity.

Seal the Chapter

Relationships can be a heavy burden. They can sometimes have us up late at night pondering about what did we do wrong. You tried your best to please your spouse. You tried your best to please your family and loved ones, and it still wasn't good enough. You have sacrificed your money, time, and your goals. You talked about your goals and dreams every day and your spouse doesn't care. When you talked about your goals and dreams, they say you are crazy; you are living in a fantasy land. When you start talking about your goals and dreams they huff and puff and change the subject because they don't believe in your dreams. They don't see your vision. If you are not careful, they will steal your strength and destroy your vision. And many times these family members and spouses don't have goals and dreams. They sometimes, most of the times are weak-willed, weak minded people. It seems like in the beginning of the relationship you made a little progress, but now your life is at a standstill. You start talking to family and friends telling them all your problems. And most of the time they don't even tell you the truth because they think that they will hurt your feelings. And you probably wouldn't listen to them anyway because you love your spouse so you remain optimistic.

You tell your spouse over and over again about the things that they are doing that's bothering you and they listen for a few minutes but the old behavior resurfaces. You have done all that you can to make it work, but your best is not good enough.

Finally, you start praying to the "CREATOR" and HE tells you. "It's time."

And you say, "It's time for what?"

"It's time for you to let go and move on."

And you say, "But I love him" or "I love her. Just change his bad ways."

And the CREATOR says in a small, still voice, "It's time."

And you say, "It's time for what?"

"It's time to be alone for a while so that THE CREATOR can and will strengthen you." And you say, "CREATOR. I don't want to be alone. Just work out my failed marriage. Work out my failed relationship. I don't want to be embarrassed. My momma told me that he wasn't no good."

THE CREATOR says, "It's time."

And you say, "It's time for what?"

"It's time to learn the valuable lessons and move on."

And you say, "What lessons" and move on.

AND the CREATOR says, "The lesson is open up y our eyes and pay attention to the signs.

When a person doesn't help you achieve your goals and dreams, they don't love you. When a person doesn't listen to you when you are pouring out your heart, they don't care about you. When you tell your spouse your goals and dreams and they start huffing and puffing and then they change the subject, they don't care about your happiness, joy and your purpose in life. When a spouse's action or behavior bothers you and you ask them to try and change it and they don't because it's who they are, and if that behavior shakes your peace, then that person is not for you. If you give your all and your spouse is only giving 50%, that's a sign of selfishness. Get out of the relationship.

We must pay attention to the signs. When a person shows you who they are the first time, believe them. If they lie to you, then they are a liar. If they steal from you, then they are a thief. If they don't try to help motivate you to achieve your goals and dreams, then they are selfish. We must pay attention to the signs so we can know when to seal the chapter of dead end non-progressive relationships.

The Four Horsemen

Malcolm Gadwall in his book, "Blink," talked about a fascinating technique called thin- sliced. It is a concept created by Dr. John Gottman when thin slicing a couple or person you should look for four things/emotions: the four horsemen: defensiveness, stonewalling, criticism, and contempt.

Contempt is the most important emotion. Contempt is when you speak from a superior plane and is very damaging. Gottman has found, in fact, that the presence of contempt in a marriage can even predict such things as how many colds a husband or a wife gets; in other words, having someone you love express contempt toward you is so stressful that it begins to affect the functioning of your immune system. Contempt is closely related to disgust. For example, if your spouse says you are nothing but a whore, or if your girlfriend tells you that you are less than a man, that's contempt.

Every relationship has a pattern, a kind of DNA. Some relationships have an off and on pattern. One moment they are together and the next moment they are separated. This behavior can go on for years.

Validation

Oprah's final show at the conclusion of the show, she said that in her twenty-five years of doing talk show TV that everybody wants to be validated. Do you see me! Do you hear me! Do you understand me!

Validation is when other people say yes, I hear you! Yes, I see you! And yes, I will try to understand you. We must get back to knowing our spouses, family members and loved ones.

I have found that we simply don't know the people who are close to us.

Are you validating your children? Are you saying to them, yes, baby I see you. And are you validating your husband? Are you saying to him, yes, baby I hear you. Are you validating your wife? Are you saying yes, honey I get it? I understand you and what I don't know about you help me to understand. I want to help you with your goals and dreams. And I see you work hard around the house and I'm going to help you. I know that you need me some "me time".

I believe if we don't get validation at home, from our family members and loved ones, it can cause us to seek validation from other people. I believe that's why some people work twelve-hour days at work, especially when they have fifty thousand dollars in the bank. Please make sure your family knows that you love and appreciate them. Validate them.

ABOUT THE AUTHOR

Albert Murphy is from Chicago, Illinois. He comes from a big family. Albert lost his father when he was 15-years-old. After his father passed away, he can remember looking through his things…his belongings. He wanted to know who he was and what he believed. The only thing that he found was an old wallet.

In 2007, Albert's daughter S'amone was born. He wrote this book for her. Albert says that if he passes away before he can teach her his life lessons about relationships, she will have this book to guide her.

Albert also wants to make a conscious contribution to his family, his community and to humanity.

Albert John Murphy

www.ingramcontent.com/pod-product-compliance
Lightning Source LLC
LaVergne TN
LVHW051352080426
835509LV00020BB/3396